We've all seen them—muddied, bedraggled, groggy from too little ~~March 4 2011~~ sleep or buzzing from too much coffee. There may be a characteristic green smear of horse slobber across the shirt, perhaps an errant wisp of hay clinging to the front of the jeans. Often, they are in the midst of per-forming one of several familiar tasks: load-bearing (hauling shavings bales, water buckets, heavy saddles); couriering (parking oversized rigs, rushing to the secretary's office with last-minute entries, running to the store for a cold drink or snack); holding (halters, helmets, whips, coolers, brushes, boots, carrots, cell phones); or agreeing ("You're right, the judge at C probably hates chestnut mares." "Yes, they should definitely dismiss jackets." "I know, I should have parked the trailer in the shade.")

Who are these hardworking, agreeable creatures? They are the ever-patient partners of horse-crazy women—husbands, boyfriends, fathers, brothers—and they are often introduced to "planet horse" and all its sweaty, expensive glory without knowing any better (or when they do know better, blatantly against their will). They "come along for the ride" because they love the women in their life, and well, those women love horses.

Now, a man on the "inside" shares his planethorse experiences, with all the bare-it-all bravery of a desperate individual trying to understand the strange world of which he's become part. With exceptional humor and touching honesty, Menno Kalmann tells of his misadventures in muck-ing, fencing, foaling, and showing, exposing the intricacies of his relation-ship with his equestrian wife (and her horses) along the way. *Women Are from Venus and So Are Their Horses* is laugh-out-loud fun for everyone—a one-of-a-kind look at the delicate balance between men, women, and horses, and a hilarious commentary on what can happen when these three (very different) worlds collide.

Women Are from Venus and So Are Their Horses

A Grown Man's Musings on the Opposite Sex in the Saddle

 Menno Kalmann

Dedication

For my wife, to whom I pledged myself

through sickness, health, and horses

Translated by Jeroen van Swaaij

Cartoons by Jeanne Kloepfer

TRAFALGAR SQUARE

North Pomfret, Vermont

First published in the United States of America in 2010 by
Trafalgar Square Books
North Pomfret, Vermont 05053

Library of Congress Cataloging-in-Publication Data

Kalmann, Menno.
   Women are from Venus and so are their horses : a grown man's musings on
the opposite sex in the saddle / Menno Kalmann ; translated by Jeroen van
Swaaij, Pen and Sword Translation Services ; cartoons by Jeanne Kloepfer.
      p. cm.
   Translated from the Dutch.
   ISBN 978-1-57076-468-4
   1. Horsemanship--Humor. 2. Women--Conduct of life--Humor. I. Swaaij,
Jeroen van. II. Kloepfer, Jeanne. III. Title.
   PN6231.H577K35 2010
   839.31'47--dc22
                                        2010030810

Cover design by RM Didier
Typefaces: Kabel, Apple Casual
Printed in the United States of America

10 9 8 7 6 5 4 3 2 1

Contents

Pardon My Dutch

The Netherlands is a tiny little country, with barely enough space to squeeze in proper housing for all its inhabitants. The remaining space is covered by highways, which we use to spend our days stuck in traffic jams. We try to manage by working in our cars, and halfway through the day, we turn our vehicles around and make it home just in time to start enjoying our spare time. After all, that is what we spend our hard-earned money on.

By the end of the afternoon and into the night is when we really get going, rolling up our sleeves and plunging headlong into club life. We go play in our drum and bugle corps, we weave baskets, renovate old-time motorcycles, produce our own soap, fly model airplanes, or we go to an astronomy club to watch the stars together.

And then there's sports, of course; we head for the gym or practice at the soccer field.

Or we visit our riding school.

I've often wondered at the sheer number of horses one encounters in this densely populated country. Everywhere you look you'll see some horse or pony occupying a back yard. Most of the smaller villages don't have their own library or first aid station, but you'll always find at least one riding school. Local newspapers are full of ads and results from some minor local competition: dressage; jumping; and pictures of horses drawing small carriages filled with elderly men wearing bowler hats.

The Netherlands is a true equestrian nation.

Sure enough, we have our wooden shoes, but you'll mainly find those in the souvenir shops, and you might find some derelict old windmills here and there as well. They're folklore, but horses are another story altogether; you'll find them anywhere.

A parallel world appears to exist alongside the regular one, and that is the world of horses.

I found out just too late—about a month after I got married, to be precise. I was aware that my fiancée visited a riding school every now and then, but hey, I have visited a steam engine museum several times, to name but an example. To each his own, I thought; people should allow each other space for doing these things.

I had failed to realize that horses are not a hobby but a way of life. Before I knew it, we had to move to some backward hamlet in a far corner of the country where no sane person would want to live. Nonetheless, there was room to build some stables, and have our horses graze on our own patch of land. That's when the real trouble started.

These days, in all honesty, I don't have any time left for work, though at the same time I really should get a second job to be able to afford our current lifestyle. Moreover, the very modest amount of respect and esteem I enjoy in the regular world just vanishes the moment I set foot in the world of horses. I am an outsider, and apparently, humility is the appropriate attitude to go with my position. There are times when I find myself lying in bed completely exhausted, wondering how on earth I got caught up in all of this. It's baffling, really—one might write a book about it....

Talking in Code-1

There is a significant complication in my life, and I'm pretty sure I will never be able to get around it. Grooming ponies since she was six years old, my wife carved out a niche in the world of horses long before I met her, cleaning out stables all week long just to spend fifteen minutes riding a Shetland pony considered too loopy to suit paying riding school customers. A childhood like that is bound to leave its mark.

There were moments when all of a sudden, without any warning, she just switched from regular conversation to speaking in some unintelligible code and it usually happened when horses are involved somehow. As she was talking day and night about horses, I thought that buying her one might stop all this twaddle. So, this is how it all began!

According to the advertisement, the horse had already been broken to some extent. If it had some mild dents and scratches, I was pretty sure we could fix it up. We might be able to get a discount— after all, my first car hadn't been entirely intact either.

The horse dealer assured us that the horse had "a nice forehand." Being a squash fan myself, I couldn't help but wonder what its backhand and overhead smash would be like. My wife went on to ask him, "Do you ride him under saddle?" A brief mental sketch resulted in a visual image, which seemed sensible, making sure that the rider remained on top of the saddle, with the horse safely underneath.

I felt pretty confident that I could get the hang of this language and I tried hard: frog, fetlock, hindquarters, and longeing, but somewhere around running martingale, I gave up.

I find myself sauntering over to our backyard arena and seeing my wife bounding around, clinging to her beloved nag: "He feels a bit lame, don't you think?" I hesitate to answer as I watch them. Who am I to judge? I'm sure she finds some of the things I like to do pretty lame as well. Later on, after unsaddling and the obligatory "That's it, I quit,

period!" she treats me to an elaborate debriefing on all the specifics.

"He's not in front of my leg, and he is constantly four-beat cantering." She's definitely lost me there; I have no clue how to interpret this. "And, when he is going round, the hind legs—they keep falling out!"

I gaze at her in desperation. Will I need to go out in the dark and search the arena for lost legs? Later on, as we sit in the car, she confides her intention of riding "forward and down" for a bit. I can only applaud such a decision, the more so because I understand at least half of it. Forward riding has the advantage of seeing what's in front of you, and going down seems wise enough as long as you're not flying a Boeing over the Hudson.

I am learning; it can't be that difficult....

Talking in Code-2

The first few times I went along to my wife's riding lessons I was fairly self-assured. Even though I was just a spectator, I was under strict orders to pay full attention as doing so would enable me to contribute to training at home in sensible ways.

But then, after a few weeks, just to confuse me, I guess, my wife and her trainer suddenly started her riding at a higher level, with new exercises and movements. Of course, these were accompanied by all new jargon as well. "Your horse is in three parts!" Now, I am well aware that horses can get sick or even die, but to my knowledge they usually do so neatly in one piece instead of falling apart into separate components.

But after a while, I was confident that I had pretty much mastered the vocabulary. For instance, I figured out that "collection" doesn't mean wanting to obtain as many horses as you can—just as well because we only have a stall and a half—but instead says something about the way a horse is ridden.

There was a brief moment of confusion when I heard the instructor mention "self-carriage." I suppose that emancipation is all well and good, but why bother driving over here if the horse and rider are asked to just carry themselves?

Then, finally, when the horse is asked to perform some move with an unintelligible French name, I am certain I hear the instructor announce that "the hindquarters are not underneath." Oh please! I think even I would have noticed that; I seriously doubt whether my wife would have managed to stay on with such an important part of the horse missing.

It has been another exciting day, lessons, handling the rest of the

horses; the usual equestrian housekeeping. This evening we are both exhausted as we finally get home.

After I've hung my coat on one of those whimsical coat hooks made of horseshoes and stirrups, brushed my teeth using the tooth-brush with the horse's head I got for my birthday, and draped my clothes over the rack made of horse's bits, I finally doze off under my blanket decorated in a straw pattern dotted with carrots, content in the knowledge that tomorrow will be my equestrian day off.

Despite the fact that my wife has spent about 17 hours with our horses this Saturday, she feels she hasn't had enough "horse" time so plans to get up early tomorrow morning and drive all the way to the other side of the Netherlands. Some large equestrian event is being organized and, of course, she can't let the occasion just slip by. As it turns out, my presence is not required. Of course, I will be allowed to review the entire affair later by means of the three hours of tape I have to record from some obscure sports channel.

So, I can look forward to a quiet and horse-free Sunday—except, that is, for feeding; cleaning out the stables; taking the horses outside; walking the one with the tendon injury around; bringing them all back inside; oh, and, of course, allowing the injured one to graze for half an hour (or it would be unfair), though he needs to be held as he is not allowed to walk around by himself; and bringing a bit of hay over to the Shetland pony, slightly moistened because my wife would definitely notice if I used dry hay; and removing the droppings from the field.

I drift away into deep slumber dreaming about...a beautiful Harley Davidson.

The Riding Arena-1

Everyone knows exactly how to get it right. The lot behind the house was going to be the "arena," and the neighbor across the street who keeps horses too, readily informed us about the local soil which, three feet below surface level, would provide the perfect footing for an outdoor training ring. An excavation worker was called in, and it didn't take him more than half a day to turn over the soil, yielding a golden yellow "floor" as smooth as a sheet of glass. How simple and efficient! Time to buy that neighbor a nice bottle of liquor to express our gratitude; everybody needs good neighbors, especially ones providing great advice at times like these.

I could hardly wait to see my wife ride in our "super-arena" for the first time. It turned out to be somewhat of a disappointment. The horse sank into the sand right up to its knees, and after a single lap my wife decided to quit. "If you're so intent on ruining the horse..." she snarled as she left to ride in the woods.

"I've got a competition coming up in one week for crying out loud, so you'd better sort this out," she muttered under her breath.

I was left standing in this desert, with nothing but my doubts for company. Even though I thought that it wasn't all that bad if you didn't stamp your feet too hard, I felt I had to do something. Turning to the neighbor for advice, he thought it strange that two adjacent lots could have such different soil types. Not to worry though; he had seen this happen before and the thing to do was just dump a layer of loam over the whole thing.

So the next day, the excavation worker returned with four truck-loads of loam, and left me with four giant heaps of clay, a shovel and

a rake. I spent two days locked in an uphill battle, wrestling my way through tons of dirt. Two bloody hands and one ruined back later, I was looking at eighty cubic meters of brown loam smoothed out over the yellow foundation like a thick layer of peanut butter on a sandwich.

Things were okay for a while. The horse managed to stay on the surface without sinking in too deep. The trouble started after half-an-hour's drizzle when we suddenly noticed that our backyard was blessed with a fabulous pond. It was a large pool, attractive enough to tempt a heron into trying it out, gazing in anticipation as it stood beside the water on one leg—would there be any fish in it?

So there I was, dragging along my soil auger as I drilled holes every six feet, trying to construct some sort of drainage system down underneath the complex sandwich of different soil that I had created so far. The blisters on my hands nearly gone from the first round, were replaced by fresh ones. Nevertheless, five hours of toiling later I had created a lovely Swiss cheese that did indeed allow the water to drain away. Of course, after a week of riding, all the holes clogged up again, allowing us to enjoy our frog creek once more. I felt no urge to ask anything of my neighbor, except maybe to give me back my bottle of booze, and I decided to ignore his wise counsels for a while.

At that point, my other neighbor, a farmer, had been watching my efforts patiently for quite a while. "Loam tends to clog up you know," he spat on the ground as he stated the obvious and prodded his clog into the mud. He went on to say, "You'll want to till this down to

about a foot and a half." He had one of those tillers and it didn't take him more than 30 minutes.

"Way too loose," my wife groaned as she returned to the woods. "Just takes some rolling," the farmer retorted. Moments later, he was traversing the arena with a gargantuan roller. When he was done, it looked absolutely perfect, and even my wife could think of nothing worse to say than "the darned horse wouldn't respond to her leg at all" (though the arena had precious little to do with that).

After a week, however, it did turn into something of a mess again, and I received immediate orders to drag the arena floor. I rushed to the tractor dealer around the corner to get a huge tractor tire. After drilling some holes in it and connecting a bright orange nylon rope to the tractor, I found myself driving our rural tank in circles around the arena, on four-wheel drive, dragging the tire behind. The kids in the neighborhood soon discovered the fairground attraction joys of hitching a ride.

Four weeks later, conditions had reverted to their familiar inaccessibility: rock-hard patches interspersed by spots where you could easily sink two feet below the surface. After again consulting the excavation worker—he should know, shouldn't he?—the entire arena has been overturned another three times, slightly deeper on each occasion using all kinds of additives: fine sand, river sand, seabed sand—you name it. I now own a professional drag, a single-tine tiller, a tractor, and one of those gigantic rollers. A solution is nigh.

At the Horse Show-1

In shock, I punch out the alarm clock on Sunday morning at 4:30. There must be some mistake. Has daylight savings ended? Am I going on holiday? Or am I having a fever and is it in fact 4:30 in the afternoon? My wife looks back at me in disbelief, only to fall back into her pillow in exhaustion issuing orders: you feed, I get dressed, then I braid. Suddenly I remember: I married a woman gone insane who uses her leisure activities to terrorize not just herself, but her entire environment.

After having fed the surprised-looking horses—that time already?—I sit clutching a cup of coffee, numb with cold. A door-man from one of those fancy city hotels descends the stairs, dressed in a ridiculous tailcoat and top hat, who on closer inspection turns out to be my better half: "Did I get my bun right?" Woe to the man who dares to make a funny remark at crucial moments like these!

Being horsey is a genetic disorder, and if you're not horsey you are suddenly stripped of all relevance. No matter how much you like to think of yourself as quite the worthy person with a decent and weighty job, and relations who treat you politely and respectfully, throughout the day of the show you are suddenly demoted to pup-pet status; an infantile halfwit who is to be shouted at and scolded, who gets to do all the nasty chores and who is apparently to be blamed for everything that can possibly go wrong.

She glares at me furiously. "Why the heck is it raining!"

I mumble an excuse as I try to crawl into my coffee mug.

"Did you pack the insect repellent?" I jump to my feet.

"Never mind, just stay where you are. I'll just do everything myself, as usual!"

We are on our way at last. She is driving—of course she is driving.

I am less than nothing right now; a deadweight that never fails to say stupid things in front of horsey people. The kind of person who is never able to answer questions about pedigrees: I think the horse is a descendant of pony dinosaurs.

No jokes allowed though; these will be severely punished at a later stage. I attempt a casual "It is early, isn't it?" Deafening silence follows. Is it nerves, or is it war? After a 75-minute trip we slowly drive into the parking lot. She turns off the engine and gives me a penetrating look lasting several moments and says, voice full of contempt: "If you screw up reading my test to me..."

Cursing under her breath, my wife is attempting to use the reflection of the car windshield to align her bun, her hat, and her eyebrows, and my "Is there anything I can do?" is met with her directing her eyes toward the heavens.

The first dressage test she knows by heart, and I nervously mumble along with what later turns out to be a different test altogether, in order to immediately provide lavish praise. "That serpentine was superb," I add to my thumbs-up, but apparently there was no serpentine in the test at all, and my wife is gazing across the showground as if she is acquainted with everyone present, except me.

I read out the second test, carefully striking a balance between submission, helpfulness, leadership, and routine. Much later, as I sit waiting broken-spirited in the trailer, the door suddenly swings open, revealing a second place ribbon along with an unidentifiable silvery object. She embraces me with a "Well read!" and I get a kiss. Once more, I am glad to have been a great support.

Accident Prone-1

I am standing in the street with a longe line in my hand, the far end of which is tied to the trailer. My other hand clutches a carrot and a whip, while my wife is controlling a horse as well as holding a bucket of grain. We are alternating stern words with sweet talk, walking ahead of Alma dangling the bucket, pushing or patting her behind. But Alma refuses to enter the trailer.

It's been 45 minutes since we started out, and we are now officially running very late in our efforts to make it to the competition. There was a brief moment when Alma had gone quite far up the ramp, but then she decided to turn around after all. I am handed a second longe line, and am now hovering 30 feet behind the trailer, the two lines in my wide and high spread arms, with Alma secured in between and my wife close behind her.

Alma steps forward, has nowhere left to go but up the ramp, discerns a pile of carrots inside the trailer, takes a huge mouthful of orange vegetables, and then backs down the ramp in bounding leaps, is surprised by the pair of longe lines escapes them and, moving elegantly, trots down the street and round the corner leaving a marital crisis in her wake. That's just our Alma. Never a dull moment while she's around.

Meanwhile, we are slowly running out of grass. Our friendly neighbor from across the street was kind enough to let the horses graze the land occupied by his sheep for a month or two. Even so, it is a well-established fact that the combination of horses and barbed wire is the chief source of income for vets, so a four-foot buffer zone had to be created using an electric fence connected

by a menacing mushroom-shaped fence charger, fiercely ticking
away in the corner.

Alma allows herself to be lead effortlessly into greener pastures—
such an easygoing horse! I am watching her stand relaxed and satisfied across the road through the kitchen window. She even starts
rolling to emphasize her convivial mood. So, it's inevitable that she
chooses to lie down right next to the live wire, rolling inward and
then out, all four legs flung over the electric fence as one of them
extends to get trapped firmly underneath the barbed wire.

I choke on my coffee as I stand and watch. The horse lies stuck,
twitching to the rhythm of the mushroom like someone in cardiac
arrest being resuscitated. I sneak over to the scene, and as I switch
off the mushroom the huge lump of flesh slowly calms down. I walk
over, careful not to startle her. Here we go again. "Keep still like a
good horse Alma; I'll lift up the wire and you can gently pull back
your foot."

In a flash of personal initiative, though—No, my wife always
claims, horses are highly intelligent animals—this particular specimen
looks at me dimly and thinks: "You know what, I think I'm gonna get
up," and as she untangles her leg, the barbed wire carves some neat
deep gashes into the flesh. As she rises to her feet, I scramble out of
the way just in time to avoid her flailing hooves in the flurry of
bounds constituting her victory lap.

"That was so much fun!" My wife is not around and I boldly
resolve to call in the vet, as by now, impressive slices of smoked
horsemeat are dangling around. He arrives 20 minutes later to find

the animal grazing away without a care in the world. As he stitches her up, he wittily remarks: "Horses and barbed wire—not exactly a match made in heaven are they?" A triumphant bill lands on my doormat two days later.

At the Horse Show-2

It is 7.00 a.m. and my socks are soaked already. The field serving as a provisional parking lot is still wet with dew. I am carrying what feels like at least my own weight in fly spray, isotonic energy drinks, a top hat, a coat, a video camera, and a folding chair, as I try to find my wife among the riders at the warm-up. This should be easy; she is mounted on a horse, wearing a white blouse and a bib adorned with a pin, hair in a bun. To my dismay, everyone present fits this description, so I decide to sit passively along the sideline.

Unfortunately, this is a national show, not a local show, which I regret.

The great benefit of a local show lies in the fact that people start drinking quite early; the beer tent breathes an atmosphere of brotherhood as men gather to commemorate their common fate—they are all losers today. In addition, "local" is always organized around fairground coziness, with music and cotton candy stalls, a volunteer grilling hamburgers left over from some bygone national holiday, and a PA abusing the sound system to drown out the inevitable folk singers and wishing people a nice day of sport despite the rain.

Local show competition riding means making the best of a bumpy field flanked by handmade signs, as opposed to the larger national shows with perfectly smooth pastures lined by fences, preferably with a freshly mown centerline.

Apart from the beer stand, though, another advantage of local competition is winning cash prizes, whereas national competitions generally award silvery objects of dubious use. The other day, we won something and I'm still unsure as to whether it's a tea tray, a mirror, or a picture frame for some huge oval portrait. I prefer cash prizes any day of the week, and I usually snatch them from my wife's hands while she is still being congratulated by the show chairman. Nonetheless, as we drive home, she will declare that all prize money should be kept in a special fund, to be spent on buying something

nice for the horses. I blankly stare out onto the road ahead. So much for a small contribution in financing her outrageously expensive hobby. A fund! Off-limits to me!

She's performing her second test, which I am supposed to read out. The rain is pounding down mercilessly and as the thunderstorm builds in force, I hear her shouting "Louder! Read louder!" as I peer at the drenched booklet. Since I can't even see all the way across the arena, I am unsure whether she's anywhere near the "M" yet, where she is to perform the movement I tell her to do.

She flawlessly salutes the judge's stand with a warm smile, water spilling over the brim of her hat, apparently unaffected by the appalling weather. The skies clear as she cools down and the test is scored. "Too bad about that one transition, don't you think?" she says. I decide to agree and say it was indeed, worthless. "Well it wasn't that bad was it?" she counterattacks.

An hour later, we stand in line with truck and trailer as we wait for our turn to be dragged out of the soggy field by the kind young man and his tractor.

Back home, as I stand cleaning my hands of the crap collected helping her get out of her boots (I was unable to find the appropriate device right away), she is suddenly behind me and wraps her arms around my waist. "A wonderful day, don't you think?" she says. "Perfect", I concur, glad that tomorrow will be just another regular Monday.

Accident Prone-2

After having enjoyed a few riding lessons on Alma, I was allowed to take her to the woods to cool her down. The mare knew the way, so I had little to say in the matter. "Walking only, remember!", my wife yelled as I left.

Of course, I couldn't resist the temptation: What's wrong with a little bit of galloping along that long, lovely straight sandy track? I searched my memory—outside leg behind the girth; but which one is the outside leg when going straight ahead? Then I decided to just give it a go, yelling "Gaaaa-llup!" as I did.

This was all Alma needed to hear. I must admit it all went pretty fast. And unfortunately, the brakes didn't work: of all that I had learned during my crash riding course, the concept of "giving a leg aid" had stuck somehow, so leg aid I gave, digging the heel of my boot into the horse's spleen with a nasty little kick.

What happened next I can only recall as a scene from some bad dream. Much to my surprise, it turned out that Alma could go even faster—way faster in fact. Incredible! I tried to hang on, and even succeeded to some extent, up to the point when disaster struck. Quite unexpectedly, an empty French fries carton appeared by the wayside. Now, you should know that Alma is not easily startled, but if there is one thing that absolutely terrifies her, it is the grim terror posed by a carton of French fries. You can drive your noisy tractor and manure spreader right her by at full speed and she won't even blink, but this little piece of colored cardboard is the very incarnation of her worst personal nightmare—especially when lying in ambush by the side of the road.

Alma responded to this situation by instantly turning around at full speed; surely a stunning feat of athletic excellence defying several laws of basic mechanics in one bold move. Unfortunately, I was wholly unprepared for such a drastic turn of events, and readily obeying Newtonian theory I was launched into the undergrowth like a projectile in a neat straight trajectory. For a few moments, I lay stunned on the ground. "Am I dead now?" I wondered. However, the bushes had apparently broken my fall as I had broken them in turn, leaving me stranded in the undergrowth with little more than a few scratches and a slight limp.

Alma, breathing heavily, was waiting for me a few yards ahead. The poor creature had had quite a scare, and let's face it, some French fries can be pretty fearsome. Now she was patiently waiting for her crippled master like a good girl.

I spoke comforting words as I walked over to her.

When I was about three feet from reaching her, she suddenly changed her mind and decided to casually trot off home, without paying me any further attention.

There was a brief moment when I thought: "All right Mr. Kalmann, you have a choice: You can do anything you want—except go blundering after her in your riding boots yelling "Get back here Alma!" On the other hand, horses running wild can be dangerous, so off I went, clumsily flopping after her in my awkward boots, stumbling due to my sprained ankle in what must have looked like a scene from a slapstick movie.

Earlier, when we had set out, the lady next door had greeted us with a friendly "Well, well neighbor, going for a ride are we?" Upon seeing Alma return without me 15 minutes later, she was kind enough to phone not only my wife, but the rest of the neighborhood as well. I was overjoyed to have all those friendly acquaintances standing on their lawns to see me dragging myself back home, covered in mud and sweat, cursing silently as I wobbled down the street. "Well, fell off have we?"

By this time, Alma had long returned to her stable to munch on some hay, convincing my wife that all's well that ends well.

Lameness

What puzzles me is the fact that a horse may be about ten times my weight, but still manages on the same skinny lower legs. At show jumping events I have regularly witnessed horses crashing headlong into heavy timber pole barriers at 50 miles per hour, or tearing straight through sturdy walls made of blocks of wood, so to me it's no surprise that this gives rise to the occasional bruising.

And, similarly, in dressage, crossed legs can overextend, making a tendon go "snap," ripping a ligament, or snugly burrowing a bone fragment into some joint. I then end up trotting some poor horse by the reins on a Sunday morning before breakfast, as the wife stands by wringing her hands and groaning: "I hope even you can see this." Next I have to observe as she runs down the street, the horse still half asleep bumping along after her. There was this brief instant where I actually did pay attention, and so I know that you shouldn't look at the legs, but at the head. High-low-high-low is a bad thing. Alternatively, you can listen: click-cluck…, click-cluck…. This is wrong too, so I arrive at my professional verdict: "Lame!"

I know what comes next. First, we visit the veterinarian. He will hold a lithotripter up to the tendon and then shoot her up with an 18 k gold injection ("You accept Visa?"). Then it's 20 minutes of walking the horse three times a day, which is convenient as even I can do that without screwing up, and luckily I had some vacation left, so my career is suspended for a bit as I walk around town on a daily basis, counting the times neighbors tell me: "It's easier if you actually sit on it, you know".

As the symptoms don't improve over the next six weeks, we

decide not to take any chances so go to a kind of commune, where girls in sloppy overalls circle around the horse holding shaking metal rods in order to arrive at their holistic diagnosis: "This horse was a squirrel in a previous life; it suffered from an unresolved conflict with its father." They then hand us some infinitely watered-down dilution—the marvels of modern technology!—and we are charged an amount that would easily suffice for surgically removing the appendices of an average-size Mormon family.

We then move on to a man explaining to us in a Polish accent the problem is not in the legs, but in metabolism, which can be resolved instantly if we buy our horse the specific feed he has been personally developing. It only costs three times as much as regular horse feed and I am confident that if everyone started feeding this to their horses, the man's problems, as well as his entire Polish family's, would surely be resolved without a doubt.

Finally, there is this man we can call on the phone. We don't even have to go to see him. He has the impressive capacity of thinking about our horse from miles away. It won't cost us a dime since it's a gift from the astral plain—and we don't even have satellite TV! Sadly, it doesn't help either. Three months later, the mares are standing in their stalls as the lame one says to her roommate: "You know what, I think that today I'll act like I'm not lame anymore; I've left them dangling long enough and I feel like competing again for a change." And they all whinny with joy.

Reproduction-1

At the risking of losing my driving privileges (as well as my car—to the police repossessing it), I sped down a secondary road at 100 miles per hour covering the last few miles home. In the back seat stood a cooler carrying a polystyrene container, which in turn held a canister filled with indistinct ooze, each gram worth eight times as much as its equivalent in pure uncut heroin. Since keeping horses is just plain expensive, my wife in a stroke of immaculate logic had become hell-bent on having another one. After all; one must safeguard the prospect of having something to feed and to clean out six years from now, mustn't one?

Earlier that day, we had taken the mare and the trailer to the horse doctor, who had a pair of gloves just like the ones you can use at gas stations these days to prevent spilling diesel all over your hands. The one difference was that his reached all the way up to his shoulders, kind of like a pair of waders for your arms. What on earth was this man up to? I was starting to get a little creeped out as his hand and wrist vanished into our sighing horse. It got worse as the elbow and upper arm followed. Cigarette on his lip, the doctor was on the verge of burning holes in the hindquarters of our mare as she moaned.

"There's a lovely little follicle in here," was his diagnosis, "you should start driving!" So I jumped into the car and sped off to Oldenburg. This would be my second time visiting Germany to obtain semen, and the sixth time the mare was to be inseminated. On the first four occasions, the load had been delivered by a courier; usually around 4:30 in the afternoon, giving me ample

opportunity to have a day well spent waiting by the window (he'll be here any time now!) gnashing my teeth in anticipation.

This was to become a regular pattern: first, get the mare to some stud to have them sniff each other accompanied by terrible noise, lots of prancing, and an abundance of roaring. Next, the vet performing his upper arm disappearing act: hurray, a follicle! Then, communication with Oldenburg in Germany and a call to the courier. To our mutual dismay, though, something went wrong on every occasion, and I was slowly starting to hope it would all just blow over.

However, a true horse lady is not so easily defeated. So another Monday morning (luckily, I never have to work…) saw me getting dragged out of bed: "She's in heat—we're off to Oldenburg!" The underlying assumption was that semen having to cover only 15 yards from stallion to mare would be more willing than semen suffering from jet lag after a breakneck drive halfway across Europe. Thus we were standing still in an endless traffic jam somewhere along a German autobahn, trailer wobbling due to a horse scraping the floor in boredom, killing time trying to think of good horse names starting with a W.

When we arrived at the Oldenburg stables, we saw famous horse ladies on tiny bicycles and stablemen in spotless uniforms as we were welcomed like guests at a five-star hotel. I could feel my wallet's heartbeat rise. A stern yet righteous-looking lady led the way as we showed our horse her luxurious accommodation with minibar, pay-per-view, and sweeping vista of the park. Very neat and very tidy—we decided that this should do the trick. As we said our good-byes and slipped our mare some spending money, we pleaded her not to stay up late, not to hit the town with the other horses, and to please be polite at all times—after all, we were on German territory now.

Reproduction-2

It had been 10 days since our darling mare arrived in Oldenburg when we were relieved by the long-anticipated phone call: "Es hat geklappt, it worked!" So we dropped everything and rushed our empty trailer to Germany. The estate, compared to which Buckingham Palace would have looked like a Bed & Breakfast, bid us another warm and professional welcome as we received our horse, instructions, and a bottle of Regumate.

Now, apparently, Regumate is a highly dangerous hormone. We were urged to wear gloves at all times, even if we only wanted to look at the bottle, and preferably, the hormone solution should be administered by me instead of my wife. Presumably, these people estimated my chances of conceiving quintuplets to be slighter than hers, but you just can't be too careful with these things. As we were driving home, my wife assured me that the thumping noise coming from the trailer demonstrated the initial personality changes our horse was showing due to her pregnancy. I was sure things couldn't possibly get any worse.

Getting the animal pregnant had been quite a tour de force in the first place, and keeping it that way would be even harder, so no stone was left unturned to incur the continued blessings of Mother Nature. We had been gathering intelligence on the Internet, and we got advice on using Regumate from three vets as well as from the German stud farm. Their consultations ranged from one small bowl a day after meals for three months, and a bottle a day for the rest of her life. This did little to bolster my wife's confidence, and so I was instructed to drop by the drugstore to get a pregnancy test kit (it's for a friend...) for our horse to pee on.

Hormones are hormones, we thought; the utterly vague test results caused us to slowly return to our previous state of panic. So off we went for another visit to the veterinarian to get a clear picture of the latest developments. Once more, the strong arm of the vet disappeared into our horse and set out to find the pot of gold at the end of the rainbow. We believed every single word he said during his questing expeditions.

We initially were shown a screen displaying at least three hundred dots, blips, and blurry shadows, to which we hesitantly exclaimed: "Yes indeed—a lovely little fetus," and headed for home with our minds only partially at ease.

After 30 days, however, we had reached the critical point at which the mare had previously rejected the fetus several times. We were gazing at the screen, armpits damp, and after some zapping we were suddenly looking at what seemed to be a weather map of the European mainland on a stormy day. Much to our amazement, there seemed to be an object in the middle with a horse's head and little legs. Overcome by emotion, we slowly drove home again; our vulnerable mare in the trailer and my wife caught in visions of knitting tiny little horse clothes as I mused about proudly registering our firstborn at the town hall.

Over the course of the following weeks, we prepared ourselves for the upcoming event. I was ordered to practice on staying up all night, and I received strict instructions on what not to do with foals. Feeding schedules were attuned, horses exchanged stables; Italian, English, and French dictionaries were consulted at the letter W for good names, and my wife has made prognoses of the dates when the foal would be able to perform the counter canter and passage. Exciting times were up ahead; we hoped that the coming months would provide some answers to our many questions and help to relieve our puzzled minds.

At the Horse Show-3

As we drive our moldy green trailer onto the parking lot, a lady with a walkie-talkie directs us to its far end. She watches us with compassion as we park among the bums, out of plain view so as not to affect the overall appearance of the scene. Still stooping from the uncomfortable ride, we perform a preliminary scan of the terrain as we try to find the lady who will relieve us of the entry fee, get a cup of coffee, and look at the notice board that lists the starting numbers.

Could they be ahead of schedule? A small riot is being fought out in front of the list of results. Desperate girls frantically circle it uttering the often-heard, "I so don't get this—just look at the differences between these two judges!" as they raise their gazes upward from their own result to the level where the ribbons have been awarded. Despondency gradually turns into rage: "Did you see that one's lousy trot work? How can she place above me!"

As I stand and watch in amusement, I contemplate adding some fuel to the flames and then resolve to control my urge. Here comes the current number one, a paragon of unsuspecting innocence. "Any results in yet?" she asks, and the others fall silent. I hear someone pulling the pin from a hand grenade. She feigns surprise as she reads her results on top of the list, and then gracefully wanders off with a condescending smile on her face. Machine-gun fire in her back—if looks could kill....

We haven't come to that point, though; our party is yet to begin. Ever since we were promoted out of the local competitions and into the national shows, we have set foot on a planet we barely comprehend. The scene is teeming with young girls clambering out

of enormous trucks. Sometimes they are behind the wheel themselves, but they are usually chauffeured by some proud father.

They make me wonder what I'm doing wrong. Why don't I own a
truck worth more than my house, containing not just a horse section
fitted with a solarium, dressing room and saddling compartment, but
usually also a living room, bathroom with a whirlpool, gym, bedroom,
kitchen with freestanding cooker, a small cafeteria and meditation
room for the attending staff, daycare facilities, and a parking lot for
three ridiculously tiny midget motorbikes used by grooms to bring
hats to the arena, returning with carelessly discarded bandages. They
look a bit like Mike Tyson riding a Falabella miniature pony. The trucks
feature steering wheels as well, incidentally.

Everything is operated by hydraulics, and the entire affair is pow-
ered by a hidden cold-fusion nuclear reactor feeding the sauna and
all four DVD players. My astonishment usually peaks when I see "Smith
Inc. – Paving Contractors" painted on the side of the truck. Paving
must be a true gold mine: Before your daughter reaches the age of 19,
you are rich enough to buy a mobile chateau costing half a million
dollars (don't think you'll be able to use it for transporting dirt and
bricks next Monday morning).

Our horse seems ill at ease walking around the warm-up arena.
"Haven't I seen you on the cover of Dressage Today?" she asks a gray
stallion. He responds by haughtily looking the other way and
arrogantly strolling off with a few steps of piaffe thrown in—and
piaffe is not even required in any of the tests today!

I need to make a few more runs from the warm-up grounds to the

mossy trailer and back to the arena again; forgot the camcorder! I briefly consider knocking a girl dressed in her show clothes off her motorized scooter and taking it for a spin, but again, I manage to contain myself. I'm among the jet set here.

A Good Night's Rest

"Click" goes the nightlight and I am violently jostled about. "I heard a 'clunk!'", my wife says in a panic. I try to save my sleep by pointing out that "clunking is all our horses ever do" as I explain away: "wooden stalls, large blundering animals with iron shoes; what do you expect will happen when those creatures stretch in their sleep?" But my wife has stopped listening. "You go have a look", she orders. "No, you go. They're your horses." This is a vain attempt and I know it. Horse ladies have incredibly strong legs and I am pushed out of the bed bulldozer-style. "I had just fallen asleep you know", is her puzzling rationale.

Cursing, I stumble upon a bright red bathrobe and venture out into the icy darkness wearing clogs and no socks. I am greeted by a few surprised horse faces: "What's the matter with you? We're trying to get some sleep, if you don't mind." I turn on the lights and the horses blink in protest over their doors. A single opening remains empty though. The yearling! As I peer over the edge of the door, I witness a scene I have heard much about, but never seen myself. The youngster is pressed against the wooden boards, legs bent oddly against the wall with his little head flat on the ground. A sorry sight. Our gazes meet for one silent instant.

"I'm stuck," his sad eyes explain, "and I can't get up."

I'd better get my wife out of bed. There are limits to my autonomous behavior, especially in dead of night. All the more so when something serious is going on that falls right into the area of expertise of my wife, backed by volume upon volume of professional literature.

I charge into the bedroom: "The yearling is cast!"

She is out of bed already, and while flying down our fourteen stairs between six expressions of "shit!" she explains that horses can break their legs this way: "You can just carry them off when that happens;" that their bowels can get all tangled up: "That's the number one cause of death among horses"; and that you run incredible risks when trying to get horses unstuck like we are about to do. That last bit of information makes me don my riding helmet, so now I am wearing clogs, a red bathrobe and black helmet as I cautiously enter the stall.

"Now what?" I ask her. The poor creature still looks at me goofily, legs all curled up and bent against the wall. I exit the stall and my wife goes in. We repeat this routine some four more times. Then, while pointing out the mortal danger involved, she suddenly shouts that we should roll him over.

"Watch out not to get kicked," she suggests, although I would prefer her addressing the horse on the subject.

"Maybe we should use a scarf," she proposes, but I don't see the added value in that. We are now both inside the stall as I take hold of a hind leg. The horse remains motionless. My wife grabs a foreleg and mumbles comforting words. Then we go "One, two, go" as we roll the surprised animal over onto his back like a log and on into the middle of the floor. He's not kicking yet, but on my guard against a quick yearling jab, I jump back 10 feet anyway, even though there's only five feet of space left. I land against the wall with a "Clunk!" Thank goodness I'm wearing a helmet.

The horse gets up, shakes himself down, and approaches me to express his thanks. Or, so I think. After eyeing me briefly—"What are

A Good Night's Rest

you doing in my stall?"—he bites me in the collarbone. He has been castrated, but it has obviously failed to hit home. As I limp out of the stables with a nasty headache coming on, my wife is petting the animal: "Did you get scared, darling?"

I saunter out and catch a brief glimpse of my own reflection in a window. Bare hairy legs, red bathrobe, and pony club helmet. If I'd seen that in my stable I'd bite him too.

Nightmare

For some time now I had had a feeling of disappointment about my wife's equestrian results, but that morning I noticed an article in the newspaper about a promising horse. The future world champion, according to the new owner. In the article I read that he had paid enough money to buy six Ferraris and a small Hummer. That made me think.

All this messing around with home-schooling the horses that my wife has been doing so far isn't getting us any closer to the next Olympics. So I decided to try a different approach. What we needed was a ready made horse, regardless of the price.

I was scanning ads in a popular horseman's magazine when a modest announcement caught my eye; particularly the part where it said "not a bargain."

This was just what we needed. I banged my fist on the table, stating "You only live once!" The cat gave me a pitying look as I dialled the mobile phone number and made an appointment. It would be nice to have it all arranged before my wife's birthday, and it was meant to be a surprise of course.

The man on the phone emphasized again that I was to pay a huge amount of money. We were talking six-digit figures here. I didn't fully understand at first, I mean, really good oysters are described by four or six zeros, but horses? Then I realized he meant the horse would cost several hundred thousand euros!

Later, as I regained consciousness on my kitchen floor, the huge bump on my head and the cat sitting beside me (what do you mean "one life only"?) gave me an idea. I would raise a mortgage on the house and ask my boss to pay me seven years of wages in advance. The rest I'd get through one of those "fast and discreet" loan ads that I found on a Russian internet site. Problem solved. Besides, the man who sold the horse, assured us the horse was an absolute hit, a priceless mare that would guarantee many victories, and if so desired, could produce offspring just as fantastic. So we would be famous—and therefore rich—in no time, which would make our two or three million investment worth our while, no question!

I put my money where my mouth was. I polished my shoes, washed my car, put on a snobby jacket and headed for the dealer, where the horse was awaiting me fully bandaged in an "a-traumatic" stable, which means no sharp objects and foam-covered walls. They're a bit like those solitary confinement cells where unmanageable prisoners are locked away for some cooling down.

I paid the man 10,000 euros in advance; the rest I'd transfer by internet banking, and as I left I tried to gain the dealer's confidence by saying: "You know what—I'll have the other horse as well, or my trailer will just keel over." Another 150,000 in euros would make only little difference at this stage.

When I got home I unloaded the trailer. The "champ" had a misstep on her way down the ramp and hit one of those nasty little hinges, tearing an ugly gash in her hind leg. Limping into her stall, she clumsily bumped her head, stood there for a moment a bit dazed, and then decided to start rolling. She ended up against a brick wall unable to roll back.

The mare was cast!

She looked at me unhappily as she lay upside-down, and though I tried half-heartedly to pull her tail, you don't pull over 1200 pounds just like that.

Me and the champ, we started to panic. She increased her thrashing about, violently grazing her legs against the walls. In desperation, I got the tractor out and after tying a thick orange rope around her hind legs, I gently started to drive. It seemed to work. Groaning loudly, the heap of flesh got clear of the wall, allowing me to untie the rope. She had apparently got very tired of all this dragging, as she refused to get up. Was that blood coming from her mouth?

A few moments later, I received a call from a mysterious gentleman with a thick Russian accent, informing me that he was the man from the internet loan and that he hoped I wouldn't find my arms or legs broken in the near future. It started to dawn on me that I was in big trouble.

As my wife woke me up, I was covered in sweat, and she asked in a worried voice: "Hey, honey, did you have bad dreams…?"
"Yeah…," I mumbled, "a real nightmare!"

Foals-1

Foaling alarms are handy little things. Over the past few weeks, there must have been at least 12 occasions when the device enabled me to run downstairs around 2:30 at night (still in my initial deep-sleep stage) for no purpose other than to observe that we have the only pregnant mare in the world inclined to sleep on her side. This animal had been inseminated in Germany, in the typical, thorough German fashion, because by now she was as round as a concrete mixer.

This time, however, when the alarm rang with a slight extra hint of panic, I wobbled after my wife, in my shorts and on one sock. We arrived at the stables to be greeted by moaning and groaning, and in a stall lay our mare, bathed in sweat trying to get her job done. Beyond her lay a moving white plastic bag, from which a head suddenly appeared.

"A chestnut!" my wife exclaimed. She had been hoping for dark brown without any white, just like its mother and father.

"With a big blaze!", she added, as the foal was trying to free itself from the bag Houdini-style. Meanwhile, I was sent to retrieve the birthing kit my wife had been meticulously preparing. Gloves, tail bandages, antiseptic, navel clamp, cotton wool, scissors, towels and a bucket with very hot water.

"The mare has to get up," she yelled at me.

"Try telling the mare," I attempted, but this was not a good moment for joking around. I followed into the stall, but the mare was far too hazy to have any intention of getting to her feet. I spent a few minutes tugging at her sweaty head, but after a while she just got up by herself. She swayed and nearly fell back over in an attempt to crush her foal

and loving master and mistress in one single stroke. The umbilical cord had already been broken, so now we had to disinfect the stump on the foal. As the mare staggered, threatening to step on us, I lifted up a hind leg of the writhing little creature on the floor to allow my wife to get busy with the disinfectant.

"Oh no—a stallion, and he's got three white legs too!" No jokes, I remembered; especially not about pushing it back in.

"He has to stand up and drink," my wife said in a panic, "or the colostrum will be gone." I saw despair in her eyes. "She may not even have any milk, just you wait and see, of course she won't; I'll have to go find a foster mare..." She went on to snap at me: "You go and get a nursing bottle from the neighbors!"

But right at that moment, the mare regained her balance, returning to her senses in the process. Turning around resolutely, she suddenly took charge. With a politely coercive shove of her nose, she pushed us out of the stall: "I'll handle this."

As my wife looked on wringing her hands, the mare licked the foal clean, which by now was crawling around. A few gentle nudges and some tender little kicks of her giant hooves sufficed to have her help her kid up. My wife came running over carrying six books, bursting into a veritable litany of things that could go wrong at this point, but in an instant, the foal was drinking with its proud mother.

When all of this was over, I suddenly realized that it wasn't over, not by a long shot. This was no one-off experience of fun and excitement. No sir! Suddenly, yet another horse had managed to sneak his way into our lives. I'd been fooled again!

Feeding

If you want to keep horses, you have to keep feeding them. This will require you to renegotiate your mortgage and to subscribe to magazines like "Equine Economy," or "Ponies & Pennies,", to gain some insight into your financial future. Back when I had allowed myself to get sweet-talked into buying a fractious beast on blind intuition, I was assured that all horses need is some grass, some water, and a touch of sunlight.

How wrong I was. Horses eat horse feed. Not just your regular horse feed though, as that contains ground chicken feathers and fish heads, or so the packaging informs us. Surely, our horse deserves all-natural feed costing 50 percent more, and before long a "divination" session made it clear that his difficult behavior was directly linked to the feed. Thankfully, there was an even more expensive brand, readily supplied by the international feed mafia, imported at exorbitant profits and distributed to helpless suckers such as ourselves.

Of course, feed alone does not sustain a horse. Regular doses of oats must be inserted; especially if you want to use it in top gear. And since horses are always pitiful and miserable, you need to cheer them up with some swill as often as you can, adding muesli, linseed, bran, and some warm water.

Now, you might be fooled into thinking that all of this makes up a pretty varied diet, but you are overlooking horses' need for hay and straw. Hay is for eating and straw is for the stall, they told me. Surprisingly, one of our horses seemed to have a very different out-look on the matter, chomping away an entire bale of straw overnight and standing next morning surrounded by nothing but brownish sludge. It appeared that hay is for eating and so is straw.

At first, hay cost me about four dollars a bale. On summer after-noons, some red-faced local farmer would come around yelling: "I'm balin'! Need hay, over here?" He'd go on to explain that rain was coming in a few hours, so he had to start baling now. He'd ask whether I'd be willing to lend a hand—just the perfect job for someone with hay fever. When we'd finished picking up the bales, drinking a soda for lack of beer, the bill was settled under loud repeated assurances that this was some "darn fine hay."

The real scare came about six weeks later when we cut open the first bale. It burst open with a "Puff!," showering us with a cloud of green mold as we tried to run for cover, coughing and choking. Anyway, you don't want to get in a fight with your farmer-next-door, so we proudly faced our defeat. A few bales on the manure pile every month would help us get rid of them, and we got another taciturn farmer to deliver a new load of hay, clearly in spite of himself and clearly more expensive.

As our straw-munching horse was having difficulty fitting through the stable door, we ordered a load of sawdust. Unfortunately for us, in Holland sawdust is not only more expensive than straw, but the poor quality manure it produces drives the farmer carrying it off into a rage, so his price is increased to match his emotions.

Fortunately, my wife had a good idea of a way to save money—she gave me a scythe for my birthday.

Now I'm scouring the roadside with my wheelbarrow laughing with joy. Free horse feed—can you believe?—and it costs me no more than four hours a day!

Flies

As a result of global warming, we are planning on a cheap sun and beach holiday in Siberia, and the next Winter Olympics are expected to be held in Mozambique. But here too, the effects of climate change are becoming noticeable. A new fly species has introduced itself; one we've never seen before.

Horses and flies. I cheerfully stroll over to the stables, where my wife is rummaging about the grooming area, and I start to read her a newspaper article about a fly infestation this early in the year. "Tell me about it," she replies, raising her eyes to the heavens. She is busy trying to squeeze our mare into a burka. It's an all-enclosing coat made of fine mesh, complete with the Ku Klux Klan mask and an infinite number of Velcro strips. This mare has summer eczema and that means even the very first tiny little flies turn into pure torture for her. She will scratch herself open until she bleeds, destroying the feed tub, salt block holder, buckets and whatever else in the process with episodes of maddening itches.

The other horses do not suffer from summer eczema, but with the present fly plague, none of them is very comfortable. After a long series of experiments with more aerosols and ointments than you can imagine, my wife has finally found buckhorn oil made from the horns and hooves of sheep and cows—something so filthy that flies head for the hills retching and heaving after rubbing it onto your horse. Personally, if I were a horse, I'd prefer some flies on my butt to reeking so intensely of death and decay any day. You can't say it doesn't work, though.

Well, it did work; right up to the moment when our oldest—and

wisest—suddenly goes haywire and bolts off into the pasture like a yearling in spite of his respectable age. My wife calls me; I will have to witness this. The poor animal is bucking and dancing, jumping on all fours, only to screech to a sliding stop and roll savagely in the grass. He jumps up, performs two immaculate pirouettes, and continues to race across the pasture approaching the speed of light. I remark: "Did you know that cows listening to Mozart in their barns produce way more milk than cows forced to listen to AC/DC?" I am referring to the rock station she always listen to in our grooming area. But of course, this is no time for jokes.

"Something's wrong with him," is her razor-sharp diagnosis. As I stand wondering whether something like "mad horse disease" actually exists, the horse has been caught and stands galloping on the spot in his stall, furiously snapping at his belly. "He's got a fly," she exclaims, entering the stall at her own peril. I struggle as I try to restrain the snorting beast. And then it happens. Just as my wife shouts "I think I see what it is" and bends over, the horse flails out, striking her flat in the chest. For a brief instant, everyone is stunned. "I've been kicked," she says, amazed. Our sweetest horse, reliable and sociable to the bone, so careful that we have him clean out the dishwasher all the time—he kicked her!

But as it turns out, it's not too bad: a bruise that will vanish in a week. And the fly is still there. "Hold onto him this time"; "Careful now!"; "Just keep him still!" I try to restrain the horse as he performs piaffe. She quickly reaches underneath his chest and yells: "I got it!"

We go outside to inspect the evildoer. A brown and red little monster with small bent front legs looking like lobster claws. My wife

hurls it to the ground and puts her foot down on it, there, you little bastard, pick a horse your own size. The insect is hardly impressed, though. It's probably wearing a body protector. I give it a try using my wooden shoe, but it just shakes its wings and gives us an evil stare: "Is that all you got, you wussies?" I try smacking it with a brush, and when that doesn't seem to work, I use a hoof pick, a rusty hoof shoe, and in a last ditch effort I swing a broom at it. The thing just lies there for a moment and then flies off, in search of new victims.

New in the Netherlands—I hear we've now got scorpions, too. Where is this going? Long live global warming. Any day now, we will be riding dressage on giraffes (make sure you lengthen your reins) and driving zebra carriages. I will be riding my bike to work in shorts in January.

Foals-2

Young animals are cute. Young horses are extremely cute. And they know it, which can be a serious disadvantage when trying to rear them. My wife has instructed me in great detail on what is allowed and what is not. Biting is strictly prohibited, and is to be punished by a gentle, yet firm tap on the little nose. Bolting out of the stables fast is even more off-limits. Even so, he abuses his adorableness to do exactly as he pleases.

Still, he has to learn at some point, or he will become an unmanageable creature. Lifting his feet when the farrier comes; he isn't too fond of it, and so he demonstrates once again that he is made of rubber. We keep his leg up for 10 seconds in an educationally responsible fashion, and meanwhile he is agile enough to lie down on the floor and relax. He considers the halter to be a pretty stupid invention. Even though it comes in 14 flashy colors, he will duck behind his mother's belly as soon as we enter the stall with it.

Walking over to the pasture isn't going at all like it does in the books, either. I've witnessed many official foal inspections at shows where the foal walks safely next to his mother, but our juvenile holds a very different opinion and just takes off in the opposite direction. "I'm just taking a look to see what's over there," as the mare, tired by it all, tries to call him back. "Will you stay around me for one minute—I'm trying to graze here." Me, I'm just glad there's no need for me to parade the mare and foal at some show dressed in a silly white jacket, as it would probably be just me and the mare anyway—the foal long gone.

My mother used to say: "You only come around to sleep here these days, it's not a hotel you know," and I can hear the mare sighing those very same words. The foal only stops by to have a quick drink and then runs off right away to go sniff some branch or jump over a wooden board five times in a row. There are moments when he actually tries to learn something from his mother, trying to copy her example. He will inquisitively stick his nose into a bucket his mother just drank from, only to discover, sputtering in amazement, that you get your nose wet.

And all of a sudden, after three weeks, he has grown a set of large and unfriendly teeth, which he craftily uses for pinching bits of skin on your arm or leg—hard. Occasionally, he will also use the teeth for some grazing like all the oldies seem to be doing, but the grass is unable to amuse him so he will just change his mind and go charging headlong into his dam again, performing a smooth tackle as he sinks his teeth into her udder and drinks greedily. He will then attempt to mount the mare with a bounding leap, ending up with his forelegs jammed against her behind as she stoically grazes on. She will move a few steps to the next attractive patch of grass, with the little rascal trailing behind doing the conga.

My wife can be brought to tears cleaning out the stables and finding little foal droppings, but to me, manure is manure. Every day of the week. And manure must be taken off the land, or horses could get worms, and the stables need to be cleaned out seven days a week. Sundays are not supposed to be a work day, but our stable duo seems to continue production regardless, so I'm ready and waiting with the wheelbarrow and pitchfork as the neighbors head for church. Animals must be be tended to every day, so I guess I won't be condemned for it. Shit happens, even on Sundays.

Jerry

My general opinion about horses is that they're not very smart. They allow us to sit on their backs, they are unable to play fetch, and I've never heard of a guard-horse or a guide-horse for the blind.

Jerry, our ill-mannered pony, is the only one ever to display some cunning every now and then. He is capable of escaping his stall, preferably in the middle of the night. Real horses have doors consisting of a top and bottom section. They stand in the doorway gazing out of the opened top part, like you see them do in the movies. However, Jerry is so tiny that closing the lower door would mean total isolation for him. We solved this by installing a barrier made of canvas, secured to the doorway by three clasps on each side.

We thought we were being nice to Jerry, but the only way he returns the favor is by shaking the clasps until the lowest one comes off and then crawling underneath like a limbo dancer. Next morning's feeding round will find his stall empty. The neighbors will hear us calling "Jerry, Jerry!" and they'll know exactly what they're up against. We will be having nightmares about the lawn across the street bereft of all plant life. Of course, it would be the kind of lawn that is trimmed with a nail-clipper, where in autumn, the lord of the manor goes out twice a day to carefully shake the trees and remove the fallen leaves with extreme care. If Jerry were to indulge himself over there just once, we could forget about all four of our annual friendly hellos. Relations would deteriorate, as they say.

Jerry had other plans, though. When outside his stall, he had no trouble with the entrance to the grooming area and made his way into the feed storage. Having arrived on the scene, he went on to knock

over all the barrels and bags of feed, in all probability under the baffled gaze of two big hairy oafs witnessing the scene. Then, having reached the Land of Plenty, he gorged himself on the grain, the oats, and the bran up to the point of bursting. He would have been too stuffed even to greet us with his usual sarcastic chuckle had we discovered him.

As a matter of principle, he then took a few moments to break some random stuff, just out of revenge for his captivity. He knocked over some bottles of medicine, bit through the water hose, and finished off by taking a nice dump in the haystack.

Pure mischievousness then led him to discover a switch and flip it with its evil little nose. "Wow, I wonder what this switch is for?" he must have wondered. The answer came right away. We have an electric water pump right next to the stables, connected to a hose leading inside. We use it to hose down the horses after a day's labor. The switch activated the pump and when we once again found Jerry's stall empty and entered the feeding area yelling, we were greeted by the Rio Grande.

It was flotsam and jetsam; our entire inventory came floating out toward us. Barrels of feed drifted past, brushes and bandages followed, and we saw riding boots and other valuable leather items floating in the distance. The stables had turned into one big swamp of half-dissolved bran mixed with hay, straw, and crap.

"Hey there little horsey", I manage to utter as once again I bit the inside of my cheek. Scratching his darling little chin, I repeat his current market value at the butcher to him out loud. Jerry looks at me lovingly as he bites my finger.

The Riding Arena-2

Dressage riders need practice. It is in the common interest of horse and rider, even though it mainly benefits the latter in the end. When Mrs. Kalmann is unable to ride in her ring, dark clouds inevitably gather over my head: "Everyone is riding in normal arenas, and here I am plodding away through three feet of dune sand strewn with rock-hard bits." I watch her ride off to the woods, "pa-click, pa-clack" down the road.

As I sit gnashing my teeth in the kitchen, my eye catches a magazine ad she has circled with a red marker. "THE solution for your dressage arena." I decide to make a call, and a friendly man on the phone explains his ability to drop off a few bales of fabric clippings I can then use to create a balanced "all-weather" arena. The bales aren't even all that expensive, so I resolve to order eight. They are delivered by truck two days later, and after having cut them open I am once again facing a sizeable pile, which once again I am to spread out. No loam or river clay this time, but a mass of red, purple, green, and brown shreds of fabric.

Two days of ceaseless raking result in a layer of snippets spread out evenly across the arena surface. Back aching, I stand and watch contently as my wife gives it a first try. It is a huge disappointment. Wherever the horse sets foot, the layer of snippets is just scraped off to reveal the treacherous sands underneath.

So I am standing alone in the arena once more, with a distant "pa-click, pa-clack" accusingly ringing in my ears as she set off down the road again. I gave the supplier another call. The good man is in the area and drops by the same afternoon. He prods his heel into the soil, tilting his head as he squints at the scene and produces a calculator from his pocket. He informs me I will be needing another 62 bales in order to establish a "homogenous" one-foot-deep layer of sand and rags. I shake my head in disapproval as I tell my wife about what I consider an absurd story, but she just says "OK" as she returns to her professional literature. I conclude that the time has come for our third mortgage and my permanent disability as I am now required to order those sixty-two bales of shreddings as well as spread them out.

I finish raking three weeks later, and despite being broken and exhausted, I watch with deep satisfaction as my wife makes her second round of the arena without complaint. Finally, after eight years of toiling and slaving, the job seems finished. But nothing is what it seems—and that is especially true when dealing with a dressage queen.

Spring has arrived and our next-door neighbor has children across all uneven age categories. It's about time they got a playground of their own, and he has set eyes upon a nice little plot right next to our arena. When he is finished, it has become a veritable theme park with slides, trampolines, a baseball pitch and eight little "goats" imperson-ating whining kids all day long. The kids under five years old play there all day, only to be joined by the other seven in the afternoons. My "Ah well, they're just kids" does little to cool my wife's temper. Their yelling does not improve the much-sought-after harmony between horse and rider, and if the latter were to go ballistic at some point, I fear the horse might get the blame and we don't want that to happen.

My wife sees a solution: "What if the arena was in front of the house instead of behind it. I wouldn't be bothered by anyone!"

I call up the contractor and he comes up with an action work plan, budget, quotation, and a contract. An excavator arrives to scrape off a layer of grass from location B into a pile. Next, the homogenous tapestry snippet/sand layer is removed from location A and neatly spread out onto location B. Then, the soil and grass turf is shoveled back in place on location A. A little rototilling and some additional grass seed will have the horses grazing there two years from now as if nothing had ever happened. The new arena is perfect. The soil relocation has made it even more uniform than before; and without any children around, too! It took me a lot of work to get there, but I get so much in return....

Breaking-1

At about three years, horses still aren't capable of anything really. They're like overly enthusiastic adolescents, having had tremendous growth spurts but not yet realizing the consequences. This can be quite problematic. We happen to have one of these happy-go-lucky types in our stables, behaving like a puppy with a tendency to jump in your lap while being bigger than any of the other horses we have around.

We have these horses around for other purposes than just helping us get rid of our grass. They are to follow a rigid trajectory of training and education for the ultimate purpose of being shoved into a trailer at 5:30 on a Saturday morning, only to return at 5:30 in the afternoon accompanied by a worn-out and grumpy groom and a cheerful rider who is the proud owner of a new ribbon and a trophy. Ahead of us lies the long winding road from a foal to a mature, number-one pirouette marvel.

A three-year old horse has only a very rudimentary understanding of longeing. One might even claim that such a horse has never even heard about longeing. I always thought horses just knew how to do it, like a dog knows how to bark and a parrot knows how to swear. I couldn't have been more mistaken. Initially, our dressage-champion-in-the-making cooperates, walking along to the arena like a good boy. My wife walks out to the center and instructs me not to make a move, which appears feasible, but soon gives rise to conflict.

"Why aren't you doing anything?"

"But I thought you said...."

"You're still allowed to think you know! In fact, why don't you

just take a hike!" And so on and so forth.

So, I try my best at doing absolutely nothing as my wife yells "Walk!" The creature takes a few steps toward me but then halts with a puzzled expression as the longe line stops expanding. After a lot of effort, he has finally made his first lap. Then, something fun catches his attention—possibly an owner holding his breath—and he decides to try a canter. Cantering is an option when longeing; it is quite common in fact. The problem lies in the fact that he does not like the idea of running in circles and decides to go in a straight line, and in this particular case, his destination is all the way across the arena, so he takes off straight to the other side like a Tomahawk missile, the flapping longe line trailing behind because my wife let it go with an "Ouch!", accelerating right up to the point where he slides to halt at the fence.

"Longeing rocks!" he snorts at me, "Again! Again!" The longe line is recaptured and he is back at his starting position; my wife has returned to the center. "You're supposed to walk in circles," she explains patiently. Despite these instructions, he keeps racing into the far corner of the arena, my wife sliding after him face down for a few yards before releasing the line, and after she has digested about a kilo of sand, I carefully suggest perhaps asking for some assistance just for this very first attempt. "Because he just doesn't get the picture," as I present my crystal-clear conclusion.

So I am to make myself scarce, which isn't even such a bad idea, actually.

I settle down in front of the dog basket and explain to our Jack

Russell that out of his vocabulary: "Woof, wiff, and Arrf," surely he should be capable of combining those words into "Wife", at least theoretically. After 15 minutes, I decide you can't teach animals anything and I give up. You shouldn't want it, really; it's unnatural to do so and therefore you shouldn't try.

I stroll back outside and hear my wife yell "Teeeeeeh-rrrrott!" To my absolute astonishment, our adolescent oaf is walking around her in perfect little circles. What is this thing between women and horses anyway?

Breaking-2

Our three-year-old horse still has to learn everything. Longeing is going along nicely these days, but some day, someone will have to ride on his back. That would appear suicidal to me, judging by how he goes berserk out in the pasture when he snaps. Jumping six feet into the air on all fours and landing smack bang on the forelegs as the rear hooves keep launching barrages of dirt into the skies. Next, it's straight off to the fence at 120 miles per hour, without deciding on going left or right until he's three inches away from it. We scuttle for cover as lumps of dirt darken the sky. "So you're planning on riding that?" I inquire as I start collecting insurance policies. Twenty-five thousand euros for permanent injury—every cloud has a silver lining. A lucky stroke of foresight on my part.

Anyhow, breaking is something you do together as a team. Step by step. The horse looks around curiously as it stands in the grooming area. Next comes the big moment. Ever so gently, my wife taps him on the back with her hand. The horse seems flabbergasted. "Have you lost your minds?! Don't you ever touch my back! You want me to smack you or something?" Right. That's exercise number one. Hand on back; at some stage there will even be a chance of putting a saddle pad there. We try blackmailing him into it with large numbers of carrots, and he succumbs. "Well, if you really think it's necessary, I'll let you drape something across my back—oh, could you pass the carrots please?"

The next week, we use all the tenderness we can muster to carefully put a saddle on; we are still in the grooming area. The horse watches in anticipation: "Amazing little creatures, these humans." After getting him to accept the saddle and then even the girth, we feel we've come quite a long way. The bridle turns out not be a problem. Gives you something to chew on. Then, things get serious. A wobbly barrel is set up next to the horse, and my wife clambers onto it. At this point, the horse is staring at the events unfolding with eyes as wide as his nostrils. My wife carefully lies down on the saddle flat on her belly. The youngster looks over his shoulder to see what's up and is unable to cope. He takes a sideward step, causing the barrel to be ejected from the grooming spot and after a moment that seems to last forever, my wife lands safely on her own two feet as the horse stamps his four in turn, while tugging at the rope. Once again, the carrot saves the day.

Finally, the moment of truth arrives: outside in the arena with a saddle on his back for the very first time. It's asking for trouble, but it's inevitable. He's standing there, flanked by my wife as he wears that odd-feeling girth when suddenly, several things happen simultaneously. The horse looks questioningly at the mirror hanging to the side. "Hey, wow, you're wearing one of these things too!" At the same moment, an F-16 jet fighter roars overhead with a thundering noise that is to make my ears ring for the next two hours. And as if to say that this wasn't enough, the long-dead fir tree at the far end of the arena decides this moment to be the perfect time to snap in half with a terrible crack, crashing headlong into the arena with a bang. Twelve-hundred pounds of juvenile energy tenses up preparing for an explosion the likes of which you've never seen. But the nag looks at us with pity. "That stuff startle you? Chickens!"

Stables

The man who was to build our stables laughed out loud: "Permit, what's that, a permit? I've been building stables without a building permit for 25 years now, and I've never ever had a single one of them taken down."

The neighbor from across the street was getting the exact same stables we were getting and said: "Applying for a permit is just asking for trouble, just build the darn stables!"

And if you really did need a permit because you planned to build yourself a castle or an indoor parking lot, you would be referred to the local cattle farmer who was happy to draw you some building plans in his spare time. So I consulted him as well, and he took me for a ride around the village in his green Mercedes 200D, chuckling as he pointed out some 2000 sheds, stables, garden houses, and even entire prefab wooden houses; all built without a permit. "You city folks will get the hang of it in time. Don't think, don't ask—just get it over with. Never fails. Coffee?"

They had me convinced. One fine Saturday, the stables contractor and his retired assistant built us a lovely wooden structure with four stalls and a grooming area, and as we were busy painting and staining it the next Monday morning, a car drove menacingly onto the driveway; another Mercedes 200D, only a brown one this time. "Good morning, building-control department. If you don't mind my asking, would you be so kind as to enlighten me about what's going on here, please?" I reluctantly admitted the man had a point. In the city where we used to live, we couldn't even mow the lawn without having obtained a permit first. I felt our position was weak.

"Of course, you could always apply for a permit afterward," he said. He might as well have said: "Play the lottery, you nearly always win first prize!" As it turned out, building first and applying for a permit afterward is not the smartest move ever. You will be dealing with civil servants grinning evilly in the knowledge that they are right and you are wrong.

We took it all the way to the appeals court. The points of discussion were the unintelligible municipal zoning policies and the randomness involved in choosing us as an example, but the severe lady judge was of the opinion that when everyone else is crossing on a red light, you still need to stop.

I then wrote to Queen Beatrix—my last desperate attempt to get the ruling overturned—but she was unmoved by my emotional letter. And the most famous Dutch lawyer who could keep any child-raping, drug-dealing mass-murderer out of jail because some comma was misplaced somewhere, told me on the phone that I had made a very stupid move here. "Nope, this doesn't look good, I'm gonna steer clear of this one."

So one morning, a letter arrived by certified mail, ordering me to demolish the stables before October 7. I was unable to fully comprehend it. I returned to our pen-wielding cattle farmer, very well connected within local authority circles, who patiently explained to me that everyone in town had stacks of those exact same letters lying around, without ever having had to tear anything down. "You big city people make such a fuss about these things. Have a cup of coffee, man—your stables will be here 30 years from now." In spite of this, I could feel Damocles' sword prodding into my frontal lobes.

Meanwhile, my wife had packed the stables to the brim. Two horses and a pony. A section crammed with hay and straw, and a charming grooming area with saddle supports, cupboards filled with bandages, soap, blankets, and a radio playing soft relaxing music.

As October 7 crept closer, threatening and unavoidable, I developed a strange nervous tic in my right eyelid. I had great difficulty imagining what would happen on this dark day in history. Where would the horses sleep? Under a bridge or in a cardboard box behind the train station? Would the horses be invited to sleep at the town hall, or should I be calling the homeless shelter for reservations? Or, redecorate our spacious living room with some straw, some mangers and a bit of sawdust? Alternatively, perhaps I could sleep on the couch from then on, offering the horses my bed to apologize for my lack of planning.

On October 6 at 5:00 p.m., I received a phone call from our inside man. "Well, it doesn't look pretty; they may actually show up tomorrow. I even got word the police may be there!" I briefly considered packing a suitcase and sneaking out. At that moment, my wife came in with her usual update on lack of impulsion and who was on the bit and who wasn't. Against all common marital convention, I interrupted her.

"We have to demolish the stables," I whispered hoarsely. We sat opposite each other in silence for 10 minutes. "Then what?" she asked.

"Then the stables will be demolished," I replied in hostility. Town Hall put me through to an unusually friendly civil servant.

"Yes, sir, that's right, we are starting demolition first thing in the morning," he said, sounding as if he were congratulating me. He was enjoying this! Start saying your goodbyes. All my creative impulses had been suffocated. After I hung up I was dazed for a few minutes. Then I made up my mind.

I called my wife and told her: "We're tearing the stables down."

If I disassembled it myself, there was a real possibility that the remains would be worth more than after they drove their bulldozer over it. I summoned three neighbors and two close friends, and two horse ladies appeared to provide physical and emotional support to my wife. We cleared out a derelict shack where firewood had been stored, and we managed to fit the pony in there. A wobbly carport that should have been gone for ages was fitted with some beams up front by the ladies, and after adding a little door, our bewildered horses were escorted in, keeping their heads down as they went.

Meanwhile, we were dismantling the stables. The pieces of the roof came off, and we discovered that the sides were made up of ready-made sections. As the ladies went to and fro carrying saddles, bags of feed, blankets, and buckets of bandages, I was busy disconnecting the water and power supply. The woman from next door came by shaking her head and carrying a large tray of snacks, and I brought a case of beer out. It seemed only fitting.

At 3:00 in the morning, all that was left were a large stack of wooden panels and some roofing materials. We went to bed, exhausted.

We were having coffee the next morning when we saw a convoy enter the street. A police car, a truck with a canteen trailer, three passenger cars, a car and trailer from an asbestos removal company, and a trailer carrying a small excavator. The doorbell rang, and the man from town hall sheepishly mumbled something about demolishing some stables and apologies—I should understand that he was just taking orders, and all that.

"Stables?" my wife and I exclaimed in amazement, "We don't have stables; especially not with asbestos in them!" Having walked around the house, the man dropped all his papers on noticing the empty spot.

"I'm off feeding," my wife said as the horses whinnied their consent. Horses just can't be bothered!

Breaking-3

When a horse turns three years old, you can ride it; it says so in all the books. He has been wearing a saddle, and my wife has draped herself over him in the grooming area, dangling down his flanks like a shot-down gangster from a Western movie being led to the gallows by some bounty hunter. That's exactly the way we feel now that the time has come. Riding on top for the very first time, in the arena. To fit the occasion, my wife is wearing a strange mushroom-like attribute on her head. "Trying to stay incognito?" I ask her, witty as ever, and therefore inappropriate as ever. A bit like the bicycle helmets Dutch people laugh at when they see Americans wear them, although they're probably not that silly when breaking a horse. If you fail to break the horse, you could easily break your skull instead.

We are standing in the arena. I have a tight grip on the suspicious-looking animal and my wife sets up a needlessly bright red crate. She steps onto it, and the horse steps aside in distrust: "What are you up to?" So the crate is shifted, and, of course, the horse sidesteps again. So I start my countdown; yes, there it is: "Why can't you keep it in place!" A pleasant kind of certainty; the kind that keeps life predictable.

After a while, right at the point where he starts to enjoy the game, we manage to get the animal cornered. Now he has no more room to maneuver, and as cautiously as you sneaked up the stairs when you were living with your parents and got home late, my wife slips one foot into a stirrup, raises herself up, turns 180 degrees, and sits down in deafening silence. The horse casually glances over his shoulder: "Are you sitting down yet or what?"

"Now step veeeeeery gently," my wife mimes, and we take one single step. Everyone has been holding his breath so far, and this gets to you at some point. After the second step, the horse produces a near-inaudible sniff: "Frrr," and before I can even blink, my wife is standing next to me. "Did he bolt?" she asks, startled: "He bolted, didn't he!" He didn't bolt, however, and now there is no excuse. Up she goes again, with a little more success this time. I am walking around the arena and the horse is starting to get bored: "You guys move like 90-year-olds...."

One week later, we are full of confidence. We're doing rounds at a trot, and even though we are using a longe line, it's going smoothly. The horse hasn't missed a single step and the helmet is still unscratched. My wife and I take turns telling each other that it's all about confidence. If you're not scared, he won't be either. Then, without warning, a car thunders by, carrying a large bumping trailer. Horse, wife, and yours truly look at each other, eyes bulging. Nothing happens, though. "You see—just as long as you're not scared," I attempt. "But I was scared", she stammers. "Well as long as he doesn't notice you're scared," I conclude.

It's all about confidence. Later that day, the horses are enjoying some hesitant spring sunshine in the paddock. Before I go to retrieve them, I hit the switch of the electric fence. To turn it off. Then again, if it was turned off already because my wife forgot to turn it on in all the excitement, I would be turning it on instead.

Authority and confidence, that's what it's all about, I keep telling myself. With one hand, I take hold of the halter worn by the sweetest three-year-old in the Netherlands, as my other hand moves to untie

the electric fence. As though struck in the back with a sledgehammer,
I receive a shock, and so does the horse, apparently. First, it lifts me
10 foot into the air ("Don't let go" I hear my wife shout), and then he is
off like greased lightning, his master flapping behind by the halter like
a ribbon won at a competition. He goes up and he comes back
down; I see flailing hooves and I can see over the treetops. I am
unable to let go due to the shock. We graze past tree trunks and
fences. Then, suddenly, my wife comes into view. "Whooa now!" she
says resolutely. The horse halts, and she takes control of it.

"This is no good for his confidence, you know. We're right back
where we started." I limp home savoring the prospect.

Electric Fence

The fun just never stops with yearlings. Ours has an especially good sense of humor. I will be standing around petting him a little and he will suddenly bite my sweater and latch onto it.

"Now what?" I'll ask, staring into that huge brown eye from up close.

"Now I've got you, and I ain't letting go."

He cheerfully watches me walk off with a fresh tear in my sweater to get some buckets of water. He knows very well that I'll be back, so he's already thinking about his next move. He waits for me with a "Check out what I can do!" It looks a bit like skipping rope gone wrong. He is standing to the left of the lower electric wire and to the right of the upper wire—now how did he do that? Then again, I hadn't switched on the electric fence and he knows it.

I approach him cautiously. I don't want him running off at this point, or I'll be collecting fence posts and wire for the next half hour. "Easy boy, easy," I try to soothe him. Now, why am I not surprised when, just before I manage to untangle the upper wire, he suddenly does race off. I can almost hear him laugh. The pony keeping him company stands sulking in a corner: "Here we go again."

Fence posts are flying in all directions as the yearling races into the wire like a marathon athlete crossing the finish line. Luckily, the wire always snaps, keeping damage to the horse down to a minimum. Cyclists look up from the road maps attached to their handlebars in amusement, and even stop to watch. The Shetland has drawn his own conclusions and is trying to find a safe haven, rushing right over the wire that now lies slack in the pasture. "I just knew we would go do

some fun stuff," the yearling whinnies as he races after the pony, out of the field and onto the street.

By now, the tourists start to appreciate that all is not well here, so they start clapping their hands in assistance, shouting: "Here horsey, here boy!"—thus only succeeding in shifting both horsey and pony into top gear. Their clapping only increases as the two fugitives vanish from sight. I'm glad to see there are still some good people around. I see the yearling make a sharp right turn into a front yard. "Please don't let this be the yard that won the garden contest three times in a row," I mumble as I give chase. My wife, drawn to the scene by the clamor, has arrived to contribute to the festive atmosphere by yelling: "What the hell are you doing!" We run down the street together, only to find the horse and the pony standing side by side eating their fill on dahlias and Johnny-jump-ups.

A little while later they are back in the pasture. I've managed to sort of tie everything together again, and now I feel it's time for a bit of education. I turn on the electric fence--one of those pre-war mush-room fence chargers; "tick...tick...tick..." as I malevolently hold out an apple to the yearling, forcing him to reach far over the wire and eventually make contact. I am waiting to hear a "Tack!", but nothing happens. It turns out the power was off.

I run to the store to get a digital voltmeter (fortunately they only cost 54 euros). On my return I discover that indeed the power has been off. "No wonder he keeps walking through," my wife argues. I swiftly purchase a new device (for a mere 690 euros); the best isn't good enough for our precious livestock. A quick analysis indicates

that there is still not a single volt running along the wire. I must be getting desperate as I grab hold of the wire myself: death or glory!

I don't feel a thing. A 10-foot earth rod doesn't do the trick either, and over at the store they suggest there may be a nettle interrupting the current. I politely reply by suggesting an alternative location to put the nettle. As I am calling the manufacturer in a last-ditch effort, I suddenly have an "equiphany." It's too dry. The horse is standing on soil that is so parched it might as well be made of cork for insulation capacity. This will never work. I decide to throw in the towel and live in the pasture for a while to have the yearling under permanent surveillance. But right at that moment, after three weeks of scorching heat, it finally starts raining. Overjoyed, I grab the wire and touch down nearly six feet away. It's working again!

Rain

I am not allowed to drive when there's a horse in the trailer. There was a time when I used to make a fuss about this; the man of the house should not be ousted from his rightful place behind the wheel. Even though I would drive as if I had to transport a load of Ming vases to some wealthy buyer in one piece, this did little to improve our marriage. "Hey, mind your speed rounding corners!", as I try to navigate a rotary intersection at two miles an hour. "You're scaring them, please be careful," she would comment while I enraged the traffic jam behind me by trying to gradually brake down from 30 miles per hour to zero over the course of one mile. After we'd stopped, she would jump out of the car: "This isn't working, let me drive."

So nowadays, I can be seen sitting in the passenger seat looking like a fool, though mercifully, I notice that very few men are actually allowed to drive at competitions. It is an accepted custom and it is an advantage in the beer stand—we're not driving anyway. Even when we're out for a spin without our trailer, I'll be approaching a crossing just a little too fast with my wife going: "Whoooa, sit, easy, step, halt!" And after we've stopped, she'll say: "Okay, and relax your hands again." The boundaries are shifting. I'll be eating grass soon.

These days, it just keeps raining in the Netherlands. Our manure wheelbarrow is half-filled with precipitation in the mornings; our arena has turned into a frog pond, and the pastures are dotted with reflecting pools. But life with the horses just keeps on turning regard-less, and competitions aren't cancelled over a few drops of rain either. You can get soaked just taking the horses inside or outside, and then there's the one with a special blanket against sweet itch that must not get wet. My wife will be heading with the horse in the trailer for the indoor arena downtown.

"You'll take care of the horses while I'm out won't you?" she asks as she leaves. Sure, it's not as if I have anything better to do with my life. So when the rain seems to stop for five minutes I take them all out-side, and now I might as well muck out the stables. Naturally, the rain starts beating down again at that very moment, and I see the sky turn from dark-brown to green.

Of course the eczema blanket gets wet, and as a deep threatening rumble follows after a flash, I start running in my spotless set of clothes, back and forth between the stables, the pasture, and the paddock, where the horse impishly refuses to go, and as a result I wade knee-deep in the mud cursing the stupid nag as I go. "Get over here you bastard!" I yell, but my voice is drowned out by the rain pouring down so hard by now that I seriously consider swimming back. By the time I've finally managed to get everything inside, the rain ceases abruptly and the world responds steaming in shock. I tell everyone to shove it and head for the bathroom to wring out my underwear. As I look in the mirror I notice my face looks like that of a marine because of my imposing mud-striped camouflage.

We're at a competition today, and I'm standing at B reading out the test trying to make myself heard over the deluge sweeping down on us.

"Shoulder-in at M," I yell.

"What?" my wife yells back against regulations.

"SHOULDER-INNN-AT-EMMMMMM!" I scream at the top of my

lungs. By now, the booklet I'm reading from is so soaked that the next tests are starting to shine through. I can't make sense of it any longer, but to my surprise my wife appears to know the test by heart. It stings a little. I've been standing here reading out like this countless times—for what? As she salutes and bows her head, a gush of water spills over the rim of her hat, right into her groin. Serves you right, I catch myself thinking. I'm not even allowed to drive, and I've clearly been reading out tests for decorative purposes too.

The gentlemen in the beer stand have reached a unanimous decision on the need to drink Jack Daniels because of the weather. I nod in agreement, dripping, and a little while later we are headed back home; windshield wipers in "Dutch Typhoon" mode.

"Nasty weather during the test, don't you think," I decide to yell. "I didn't really notice, to be honest," she says. The opposite sex in the saddle—mounted human females are strange creatures indeed.

Snow

Yay, it's snowed! Our dogs cheerfully run out, only to slam on the brakes and shriek to a halt right away. What the heck is this? The youngest one has never seen snow and scuttles about in disbelief. The older one stands shivering as he waits, thinking: "Oh no, I just know he'll start throwing those icy balls for me to fetch...."

Oh how lovely and romantic the world looks covered in snow. It brings about so much joy and fellowship in everyone! My musings falter as my wife barges out with a face as long as a fiddle, calculating and scheming as she decides which horse goes where, why, and especially how. I smell trouble. Last year we spent hours circling the arena in our 16-year-old Nissan Patrol; her behind the wheel and me sitting in the back next to a giant bag of salt, trying to cover the snow-covered floor surface using my purple and corroded hands.

"You've been here already," "I know but there's some snow left," "Yes, it takes a few minutes and you're driving pretty fast," "More on the track," "We've got half the bag on it, jeez, drive on will you," and so on. As a result, the arena remained covered in snow, with the occasional tiny little puddle of mud that froze right back overnight.

We put the horses out in the field for lack of alternatives. Eight steps away from the stables, they suddenly seem a lot bigger, swaying around like acrobats on stilts balancing on small instable balls. My clogs bring about similar effects and as a consequence I twist my ankle three times as the horses only dare inch forward in tiny effeminate steps, now looking like sissies on top of their acrobat image.

My wife rushes over in alarm. This is irresponsible. Insanely dangerous, so we return to the stables. Rubbing two jars of grease into their hooves proves ineffective, and I try to brighten up the situation saying: "Well, it is some pretty hard-packed snow." "We should have bought those thingies," she snaps. I quickly work out the costs of outfitting all of our horses in those convenient little snowshoes, which of course will break or get lost before the next annual one-and-a-half-day snow

period this globally warmed country ever gets to see. It amounts to a sum that would nearly suffice for installing under-floor heating in the arena.

Ah well, the snow has its pleasant sides, too. Simply tie an old wooden sled behind a short fat Shetland pony and cruise your grown man's body across the park on it. It's tons of fun, and Jerry likes it too. After almost every corner we turn, I can be seen dragging behind the sled face down in the snow like a scene from some jolly family film. "Whoa Jerry, easy Jerry," but Jerry seizes his opportunity for revenge; "You were the one who wanted to go in the first place...," and I return home shattered but with a deep sense of satisfaction. In the distance, I see my wife engaged in a brave attempt to do "something" with a horse after all—in the middle of the road if necessary; it's relatively accessible a few hundred yards down the street.

A huge truck scattering salt on the icy roads passes by once again. The horse stares incredulously at the large snorting yellow monstrosity as it passes him at a few inches, salt sweeping in all directions. The animal decides that the best course of action is probably to go stand on his hind legs for a bit and bolt off toward the woods. He vanishes behind the horizon along with his rider.

"C'mon Jerry," I nudge my Shetland back into motion; "They'll be back...."

Soon enough, everyone is home, battle-worn and slobbering their buckets of warm swill or glasses of wine, respectively.

Riding Lessons

I've recently picked up my riding lessons again. Just like the elderly should have to be retested to keep their driver's license on a regular basis, so I need to brush up my horseman's basics. It's been four years since I actually rode on horseback. I have been forced to let go of my pleasure riding horse. He was our first retired dressage horse, and at some point he just couldn't go on. Arthritis and creaking joints made the poor thing groan in agony at every step.

Without hesitating, I called the vet and drove over right away. The slightly sedated horse out on the clinic parking lot, the syringe, and then that huge mound of flesh on the ground, quickly covered with a sheet of canvas. My wife hadn't come along. She just stayed on the couch in apathy and since I'm the man I exclaimed: "I'll handle this." After all, that's what guys are for.

Even so, I must have been a menace on the road as I drove the empty trailer back home. I could do little but watch the oncoming traffic appear like vague shadows through a veil of tears, and when I noticed I was sobbing loudly as well, I had to pull over. What a lousy job; I'd rather clean out 16 stalls in a row.

Anyway, this left me with nothing to ride since the new horse was being rigorously drilled by my wife, and the even newer horse was still a bit too frisky. Both of them settled down after a while, but then they spent the next two years taking turns being lame. So I was unable to ride, although I was allowed to walk them both every day, which is tricky because horse legs are much longer than my own, and this makes them take much larger strides, causing me to bounce after them like an idiot. The routine was walking around in hand, resting in

Riding Lessons

the stable, warming up, then trotting in the street to see if any progress has been made: "Can't you see he's lame! You still can't tell, can you?"

So in went another impossibly expensive gold injection, a regimen consisting of hosing him down six times a day, and then more resting in the stable, right until he recovered as horse number one started limping again.

They say you never forget how to ride a bike, but that's just because you're doing it all yourself. Forgetting how to ride a horse is easy; especially for me, because the horse was doing all of the riding and I was just hitching a ride. If he was "on the bit," it was a matter of reflexes that had nothing to do with my input.

Now, several years later, we suddenly have two horses we can ride out at the same time, which is fun: I love illegal "racing" In the woods. Let's see if we can evade the ranger and scare some unsuspecting deer! On our very first outing, however, my horse kept his head up and watched the clouds all the way, and my wife complained about me flushing six years of training down the drain, so I had to return to taking lessons in the arena.

"Heels down, hands together, and gentle with the reins as if you're holding a sponge. Stay seated; turn your buns into jelly! Don't keep letting go to the right, he's leaning on your left hand! Inside leg; outside rein. On the bit, right there, good, did you feel that?"

I reply with a docile "Yes," because I just want to get my certificate fast and get back out there.

Clipping

We have been getting along pretty well lately. Musing in the mild spring sunlight, it occurs to me that our last major crisis is six months behind us already. Clipping in autumn! That never fails to produce at least one weekend of conflict over at the Kalmanns. It all starts with me having to take the clipper blades to an ancient man in the village, who is the only person left in the Netherlands with the knowledge needed to sharpen them. The thing is, they need to be slightly curved, and therefore they should be sharpened on a slightly rounded whetstone. Fortunately, the man is so archaic that he charges outdated rates in last century's currency: "Two Guilders will be fine, son," and so I slip him two euros.

After I get the blades back, it's time for the fun to start. "Please stay out of the way or you'll unsettle the horse," my wife threatens. This job demands a level of concentration you can almost sense like the humming of a high-voltage cable.

"Will you just help me out here—he won't stand still," is the command summoning me back to the front line. I hold the creature in place and an elegantly flowing white line is chalked onto one flank. It seems this one will only get a trace clip. Now another line is required on the other side; preferably with a similar pattern. This proves to be more difficult.

"Is it symmetrical?" she chants as she runs around the horse in circles. It's quite hard to see both sides of a horse in a single glance. I comment that if you can't see whether it's uneven at this stage, you won't be able to tell after clipping it either. For a moment, my wife looks at me in astonishment: "Sometimes you're such a big moron!"

she says contemptuously, followed by her muttering something like "I'd better do this myself anyway...."

No matter how rigorously I am shoved aside, though, I am called back in no time: "Hold tight and shut up."

The moment of truth has arrived. She turns on the apparatus and sinks the knives into the thick layer of horsehair. Nothing happens. The hairs are shoved aside a few millimeters, but that's about it.

"I thought you'd had those razor blades...."

"I did," I parry her accusation.

"Well that's a pretty bad job then," she concludes, pressing the machine into my hands. I turn a setscrew on top of the device, put a drop of oil in, and try again, deforesting a sizeable section of my lower arm.

"It's working!" I cry out in excitement. She snatches it from my hands and starts clipping. It is indeed working now and large swaths of brown hair drop to the floor. This is going well, but then again, this is our oldest horse and he isn't bothered by anything.

We have another one, and he is as scared of the clipper as the average teenager is of the dentist. This results in tremendous stress; not just for the horse, but for our entire household as well. My wife came up with an elegant kind of therapy to let the horse get used to scary noises, and so I run off to get the dustbuster. She doesn't actually switch it on, though; she just runs it along the animal's flanks making soft industrial noises as she goes: "Bzzzzzzzz, you see, nothing to be scared of, bzzzzzz, brrrrrrr."

The horse looks around suspiciously, as he has a pretty clear idea of what will happen next. Then comes step two. The dustbuster is switched on. Blind panic follows instantly. The horse jumps 12 feet straight into the air, stoically disregarding the fact that the stable roof is only eight feet high.

This isn't going to work. We're lucky to have an acquaintance nearby, a vet who doesn't mind dropping in with some sedatives; a little shot that will get the horse mildly stoned. In contrast to most Amsterdam backpacker tourists though, he doesn't appreciate the narcotics at all. Head hanging down to the floor, his lower lip is drooping ridiculously low as he stands looking thoroughly unhappy. In addition he starts sweating heavily, which isn't making clipping any easier. Damp tufts of hair sail down. The result looks a bit like a featherless turkey plucked by a one-armed amateur. He has become a mass of stubble, wet wisps of hair refusing to come off, and a few long pinkish stripes in places where the knives went a little bit deeper than intended.

With one side finished, the horse needs to turn around so that the other half can be reached. Slowly and on wobbly legs, he takes a few half-hearted steps until suddenly the radio stops and all the lights go out, leaving us in the dark. I notice some tiny sparks fly out from under one of his horseshoes. That seems undesirable. I hurl myself at the wall plug and pull out the cord at supernatural speed.

"Hey, take it easy, you're scaring him," my wife admonishes me for my reckless heroics. She doesn't have a clue about me rescuing her little darling from electrocution two seconds ago. I triumphantly show her the two halves of the power cord, neatly cut in half by the horseshoe. But as I anticipate her falling into my arms, crying in gratitude, all she does is mutter: "If you would just turn the power back on, you could go fix the cord. Be quick about it though, or the sedatives will run out." It's a race against time: find a connector strip; fix the cord; clip; randomly twist the setscrew on the clipper—as meanwhile, the horse is slowly regaining consciousness and growing restless: "Heeey, man, what's going on here, man...."

Later that evening, as I am shaving my chin, my wife is in the bathtub reading a horse magazine. "Oh my, some of these horse women are such incredible bitches..." she snorts.

In the Trailer

It's raining so hard that it appears as though someone is standing on a stepladder like on some B-movie set, pouring water down from a sprinkling can. I get a call from my wife informing me that the trailer will not move an inch. Having arrived on the scene, I stand around kicking the wheels for no good reason. My wife says: "The trailer brakes are stuck on" and without even wanting to make a point, I reply: "Yeah, only the brakes are off," ostentatiously fiddling with the brake controller. Traffic rushes past on both sides, spraying huge fountains of water over our heads, and since I've become soaked to the bone anyway during the two minutes I've been out here, I decide something should be done. Circling the trailer shivering is unlikely to bring about any solutions.

People we know pull over and roll down their window just enough to inquire: "Breakdown?"

"Yeah, the brakes are locked-up" my wife yells back through her wet strands of hair.

"Bummer," they reply cheerfully, but traffic coming up from behind honks and they have to move on. I take off my good coat in an attempt to keep one thing clean at least, and in my shirt I lie down flat in the dirt and shove myself underneath the trailer until I reach the stuck rear wheel. As I reach it, I feebly slap the brake drum a few times, adding a load of black grease to my soaked and muddy appearance. Getting back to my feet, I ask her: "Please try again...," but there is no way of moving the wheel.

By now the horse is getting impatient. All this fuss around him, the busy traffic and then my wife trying again, just moving the trailer forward and back a bit.

"We need a new trailer," my wife exclaims angrily, "it's coming apart." By this she is referring to another incident earlier this week. Without any clear reason, the side door suddenly fell out in the middle of some village, landing on the sidewalk after being dragged along the pavement for several deafening seconds. My wife pulled over, ran back 200 yards, picked up the fiberglass door, and then ran back to the trailer carrying the panel under her arm like some triathlete carrying a surfboard, where it was deposited next to our puzzled horse peering out through the newly created side window.

The next day was competition day and we set out in a borrowed, rather small trailer. Driving through our village, we usually feel slightly embarrassed by our large car/large trailer combination, but after arriving at the show's parking lot we are inversely embarrassed by our insignificant equipment. People look down from their huge trucks with pity.

"Just win; that'll shut them up," I attempt to boost morale, but the procedure has already been set in motion. Saddling up has to take place inside the trailer as it's still raining cats and dogs. This job in that small space always makes me feel like one of those guys building a ship in a bottle; only they have enough time to get it done. It's a perilous situation; the saddle pad is on the horse's back, so now we'll need the saddle, but in order to do up the girth you need to get next to the horse and of course, the moment you manage to squeeze yourself in there he will start leaning comfortably against the wall, preventing you from breathing and crushing all hopes of uttering "Move over—mooo-ve o-verr!"

A little later, I am absent-mindedly recording events on tape with a few bruised ribs and a black and blue toe—I wonder who could have stood on that now?

"How did the pirouettes look?" my wife asks as she rides the steaming horse back into the cool-down area. "Awesome," I hope, because I just can't stomach an encore discussion about "blind" judges all the way back home.

When we arrive, the horse proudly enters the stable. "Where've you been?", the others ask. "Ah, you know, took a little ride, did a little test—the usual," he answers sagely, relaxing as he takes a good, long pee.

Freestyle

Today, after a two-hour drive, we've arrived on the competition grounds. Once more, the place is crawling with friendly volunteers wearing bright orange safety shirts they borrowed from some cousin working on the roads directing us to our spot. Of course, this is accompanied by a great deal of unnecessary chatter over the inevitable walkie-talkies. We see a line of parked trailers and assume we should park at the end of it.

"Hang on, wait here please. Jack, got any space left there?"

The walkie-talkie replies with a barrage of static: "Let me see—yep, send 'em over, they can fit in right down the line," and we drive over to where the other end of the walkie-talkie is waiting for us. "You can park down at the end of the line!" he screams loudly and, by now, quite pointlessly. We are parked alongside a trailer in which someone has started a serious renovation, judging from the thumping and bumping noise reaching all across the grounds. An elderly man wearing an overall comes out yelling "Stop it, you idiot!" but the horse happily carries on and by now it sounds like he's skipping rope inside. The man trudges off, resolving to set fire to the stub of his cigar instead.

Today's schedule includes a freestyle test. Here, my advanced music programming skills come in handy, as I have cunningly pasted together a merry composition, giving me the feeling that today I will be making a real contribution at last.

Before my big moment, a regular test has to be read out, but my heart is not in it. I chant it out routinely. I am not really paying any attention, because it will be my turn soon. My wife has finished

saluting and I run off to the arena where the freestyle class is about to start. I solemnly hand over my CD to the man responsible for today's technological aspects from his camper. He too has an important task to perform.

"Don't play it too loud," I add hastily, "but not too soft either!"

The man raises his thumb. We share a moment of deep understanding. And today, I get to play a part. In all honesty, I feel that today's trophy, or whatever prize it is, is half mine as well. It takes two to tango!

The man in the camper has his finger on the button. My wife is positioned next to the arena, casting away her riding whip and routinely raising her hand as she should, apparently. Nerve-wracked, I look from my wife to the CD button operator and back again—is communication working? Then, the music starts, and I almost can't believe it. It's happening! My music resounds triumphantly across the show grounds! My wife enters the arena, halts right where the music pauses—who'd have thought!—and breaks into a trot.

I creep over to the camper. I think the volume could go up just one little notch. No harm in that. Thumbs up again. This man and I—we are on a higher plane of understanding. My wife turns left and carries on along the track in what is supposed to be a shoulder-in. At that point, however, from two feet away, the horse passes by the now slightly distorting speaker and is scared silly by the warped noise it emits. From there on, the test looks very much like a rodeo show.

Initially, my wife tries to make it look as if she was planning on a circle, but then the horse rears up and refuses to leave the relative

safety of the corner they're in. A desperate struggle ensues, but the speakers now pose an invisible yet insurmountable barrier to the horse. I stand jumping furiously in front of the camper window, trying to get the attention of the sound engineer by my gestures, but he was deeply involved in rolling a cigarette and oblivious to events unfolding outside.

"Cut it off!" I signal maniacally, and only after silence has returned do we succeed in dragging the freaked-out horse from the arena. As we drive home, I switch on the radio from the passenger seat, but my wife immediately punches it off again—no music for now.

Stallion

Ever since I was a kid I knew to "never look a gift horse in the mouth." Over the years, I've learned that if you've actually paid money to buy a stallion, you'd best just punch yourself in the mouth instead. Keeping a stallion isn't easy, and knowing that doing so is actually costing you money does little to ease your burden. I remember vividly the night my wife dragged our home-bred foal from the mare that bore it; after having expressed her disappointment about his color, blaze, and asymmetrically white legs, she raised her eyes to the heavens and exclaimed: "And it's a colt too!"

At the time, I didn't see the harm in that; personally, I could easier identify myself with stallions than with mares, but now, about a year-and-a-half later, I have a pretty clear idea of what she meant. Basically, you only want a stallion if he has a certificate that clearly states the horse has been approved and allowed to clamber up the rear end of some leather artificial horse to make the owner a rich man. You then have an officially licensed breeding stallion, but I hear that isn't easy to achieve. Not a single hair must be out of place; manners must be immaculate; legs intact and straight; bones must be perfect; and in addition the stallion must have three superb gaits, excellent jumps, and bring in the Saturday morning papers as well.

Meanwhile, our yearling has become a full-fledged stallion. He shares his pasture with the Shetland that he harasses relentlessly, so we've come up with a trick to protect the pony's chastity and honor. One corner of the field is separated from the rest of it by a piece of wire the Shetland can just squeeze under, though the yearling is too tall.

The downside of this otherwise successful measure is that I get to serve as the stallion's playmate now. As soon as I enter the pasture carrying two buckets of water, I receive his full attention. I back away and the young fellow walks after me with floating strides, head high up in the air, ready to make that bounding leap and land on top of his master. The look he gives me isn't one of anger really; saucy is a better description. I keep facing him as I try to empty the buckets behind my back, and without losing sight of him before me I elegantly miss the water tank altogether.

He needs some extra feed at the moment, as there's not much grass left in our pastures. Though, at this time, feeding has to be performed using a lead line with a chain—and a whip—because he will go berserk as soon as I dare to enter four paces into his territory carrying a bucket of feed, showing the insolence of emptying it into his feed tub. Imagine me not even having the courtesy of surrendering his meal to him immediately without any further resistance—let alone carrying it around with me, heaven forbid! He cannot tolerate my impudence any longer, so he prepares to charge me, bull-style. Even though mercifully he doesn't have horns, a head butt will be painful enough.

So we decide to get it over with. The stallion shall be a stallion no more, and the veterinarian, responsible from birth to grave, stoops down beside the grievously insulted little horse as he stands kicking out violently at anyone foolish enough to get within 10 feet: "We'll see who's disabling who here!" In spite of his brave resistance, however, medical intervention must take place, and therefore, testes must be

anesthetized. A little later, when it's all gone numb, the matter is settled nice and easy. We hear a clip, a crack, and a snap, and suddenly two sedated balls are on the floor.

"Now you're a gelding." I try to smooth things over, "That's fun in its own way."

The next day he's back in the pasture, racing at unprecedented speeds and once again landing smack bang on top of the Shetland who flees into his panic room. The yearling is not prepared to leave it at that and resorts to galloping pointlessly from end to end and back again. As he does so, we see the feed tub and water tank get launched into the air producing horrible noises. "He really turned much friendlier," my wife says, beaming.

I'm calling in the riot police to feed him later.

Moments of Peace

The sound of a stable full of horses just finishing their meal. The satisfied scraping and smacking. These sounds will instantly heal you of any stress or burnout. "Chomp-chomp-crunch-chomp," interrupted occasionally by a quiet snort: "Bhrrr." Sometimes, I just grab a chair and sit down to enjoy the peace radiating from the scene. A stable full of contented horses, brave spring sunshine on my face, and I catch myself thinking that keeping horses is not that bad after all.

My wife is off to some contest to size up the competition; she is assessing her chances of winning when she will be starting at this level. So, I have the kingdom all to myself. I've done a high-speed round of stable-cleaning earlier in the afternoon, mainly by loading fresh straw on top to trick her into thinking they have actually been cleared out. It looks comfortable and therefore industrious.

Tonight, she will cheer about "Oh, how nice and clean your stables are," as she takes turns stroking all the horse noses, meanwhile giving the scene a highly critical inspection in spite of herself. Have all the halters and boots been removed? Why is the lead line with the nasty little chain not there? Did I bring in that mischievous, and as such unpredictable, two-year-old without the chain under the chin? And crossed the street! Where cars race by! And where he could easily break free if there's no little chain under his chin when you're bringing him in!

But anyhow, he's safely inside his stall—I managed by using an ordinary lead line simply because I couldn't find that one with the chain right away. Now that my wife is about to return, though, I decide to go find it anyway. This turns out to be quite an operation

and in the end I salvage it from some pool of mud. I swiftly put it in place near the stall of our skittish little gelding. That's one less piece of evidence to be used against me.

When dinner's finished, they all rummage about for a bit, drinking a little so that the water feeders make gurgling noises in a random pattern. Our lumbering giant decides he's calling it a day and lies down. Just a little after-dinner nap. The rest of them languidly stare out over the fields.

Our eldest mare has an itch on her butt and is enjoying a good scratch against the wall. She is unable to reach the spot; it's just like that itch under your foot where you can scratch all you like but you'll never reach it because it's located somewhere underneath your calluses. The mare stamps her foot down hard repeatedly, but even that doesn't relieve her of her itch. The dog and I take it all in with quiet satisfied pleasure; tiny ripples in this pond of idyllic grace. The mare turns around resolutely, propping her right buttock up against the water feeder and grating it back and forth briskly. She groans with delight.

Then, I hear a cracking noise followed by a bang, and the next moment I see a powerful jet of water reach right up to the stable ceiling. The mare scuttles off to the side wall in mild embarrassment as the other horses festively gather around to watch the show. I sit there stunned for a moment, vainly hoping time will turn back and make it all go away. Of course it doesn't, and I see sawdust start to trickle out from under the door demanding an intervention. Cursing, I search for the water main in the basement—where I still haven't changed the light bulb; I shut off the gas and all the other mains I can find in the dark. Finally, the fountain in the stables subsides. I've managed to evacuate the mare, and now she stands beaming in the grooming area: "That was cool!" A few yards away, I'm shoveling wet sawdust in my green jackboots; dripping shovel plunged into a wheelbarrow getting heavy fast.

"What on earth are you doing?" I hear a voice behind me say. My wife got home. She can't find her mare and I trudge around the stables trying to explain what happened. She has just finished a lightning inspection run. "Don't tell me you brought in the gelding on that rusty old chain!" she bellows. And as she inspects the chin of the horse uttering soft comforting words, I run the sloshing wheelbarrow up the ramp to the manure heap. The sheer weight makes me capsize and I end up stretched out in horse shit, the wheelbarrow slowly emptying itself over me as I lie there.

My wife hugs one of the horses and says: "Now what is that silly man up to this time?"

Vacation

"Stop!" my wife screams, and I hit the brakes hard. I knew getting ABS was a good idea. As we grind to a halt and the air fills with the stench of burned rubber, I look around to see what went wrong. Did I hit someone? Did I overlook a car approaching in my blind spot?

"So what's the matter then?" I ask.

"Donkeys!" my wife exclaims as she sits backward in her seat pointing at a meadow through the rear windshield.

We've been on vacation for four days, and that's a long time to go without horses: too long, in fact. So we have to pull over at the mountain trail and get out to pet donkeys and discuss the alignment of their hooves. "This one could use a farrier," she commends sternly. You should let go and relax on vacation. Take a break from the everyday run of affairs and escape your routine: the inevitable schedule of feeding, riding, feeding, cleaning, etcetera. On vacation, you're supposed to forget about everything except a glass of wine in the sun and what in the world you will be having for dinner that night.

But switching from horses to no horses in a single day is just too cold turkey for my wife. A shame, since we desperately need some time off. All the more so because of the final weeks before our departure; we've been doing hard-time.

The extra chores just keep on coming and new tasks have to be contracted out. All the horses are going on a sleepover; that one can't stand this one, and horse A can't sleep without horse B, resulting in hours of puzzling over who goes where. Then they all need to be transported to their temporary housing, accompanied by long lists of instructions. This one has "that tendon" and so is only allowed to do some walking—on a leash that is. The next one is absolutely not allowed to go out without protective socks because his darling brother will kick him senseless given half a chance. Then there's the multitude of ointments, oils, powders, vitamins, and other ridiculously expensive supplements to be hauled along in neatly labeled jars stating who gets what, and when. As soon as we finally have everything where it should be, my wife starts sniveling about missing her horses.

"Let's go take one last look?" she begs, but it's only been 30 minutes since we dropped them off. "We just can't do that to those poor souls," I shout.

"What if we just take a look from the road, so they won't see us?" I refuse to go spying on my own horses and besides, we need to get up and leave at 3:30 in the morning.

As soon as we are out on the highway, the phone starts ringing. The hands-free kit fills the interior of the car with a "I hope you guys haven't left yet?" My wife loses consciousness and I burn skid marks into some German parking lot with my heart pounding in my throat. It appears one of our horses has a bit of snot running out of his nose. "I'll just call the vet over to have a look," is the suggestion, and the problem seems under control for now. I can see my wife is in anguish.

"Are we going back?" she keeps asking softly.

"No," I reply. Just for this one occasion, I'm taking charge.

As we are taking a walk through the Alps a few days later, I briefly imagine that she has managed to take her mind off the horses for a moment, as she hasn't spoken for a while now.

Just then, she grabs my sleeve and says: "Look, that would be a great spot to put the horses," pointing to a slanted piece of dirt enclosed by some rusty barbed wire. Some picturesque ruins are to be turned into a stables complex, and we are to occupy a huge, bright green house in turn.

"And if you called in a bulldozer, that plot beside the river could easily become an arena."

Apparently, I'd be retired by that time, and I like that idea.

"And if you only manage to make a square halt, you've made it here into the national team", she cheers.

"Sure, OK, I'll start moving stuff out here tomorrow," I attempt to put things into perspective.

Arms entwined, we walk on in our musings. As a huge manure heap appears in the distance, she awakes with a start: "And here we could..."

"YES I KNOW!!!" I interrupt her and drag her off in the opposite direction.